DEXTERITY STUDIES
&
EXERCISES
For
The Clarinet

Book one

Kinesthetic Memory Studies

Order this book online at www.trafford.com
or email orders@trafford.com

Most Trafford titles are also available at major online book retailers.

Printed in the United States of America.

ISBN: 978-1-4907-1080-8 (sc)
ISBN: 978-1-4907-1079-2 (e)

Trafford rev. 08/02/2013

 www.trafford.com

North America & international
toll-free: 1 888 232 4444 (USA & Canada)
fax: 812 355 4082

I wish to gratefully acknowledge the many contributions of students and colleagues, who listened to the idea and supported the process that brought it to realization. Special thanks are due Dr. George Allen who took the time to review several drafts. His comments and suggestions were always very helpful.

Finally to *B.M.J.*,
Valdea D. Jennings, Ed. D.

Table of Contents

Introduction

The studies in this book are designed to facilitate the development of *automaticity.* Automaticity refers to the ability to perform movements and sequences of movements that are executed independently of volition and accomplished unconsciously through force of habit. The exercises in this series of books are designed to facilitate automaticity through mindful practice. Herein, mindful practice refers to the use of *kinesthesia,* (the sense that detects bodily position and movement of muscles in this, case the fingers), to facilitate the development of muscle memory. To this end, the book contains a large number of short, repetitive *memory* exercises that are designed to be played at a speeds ***SLOW enough*** to allow the student to focus attention on the *movements* that produce each sequence of notes *not* on the notes themselves. These exercises are referred to as ***Kinesthetic*** *Memory* ***Exercises.***

Kinesthetic memory exercises are constructed to be short enough to allow the student to perform them *slowly* and repetitively, without reference to the notes. As an example, the student should *slowly* play the first five notes of the C major scale, beginning with middle C (C4), up and down (1,2,3,4,5,4,3,2, etc.,) until the *movement* between the steps,(not the notes of the scale) becomes the focus of attention.

The primary goal of kinesthetic practice is the memorization of the *motion* that produces each sequence of notes by establishing and strengthening the connection between the *sound* of the sequence and the *motion*, that is, the specific series of finger movements that generates each specific sequence of sounds. The studies in this book are *not* a substitute for basic scale and chord studies. Basic scale and chord studies (e.g., Klose, Stark etc.) are a necessary prerequisite, since the ability to *hear* (i.e., correctly recognize) the precise sound of each sequence is a necessary precondition for reproducing it accurately during kinesthetic practice. Any note sequence that needs to be mastered can be organized into one or more Kinesthetic Memory Exercises.

The first series of exercises is focused *primarily* on the left hand. To this end, some of the instructions for practicing the first sequence of exercises are offered only as *suggestions* designed to facilitate the **temporary** isolation and strengthening of the left hand. Also, while practicing these early exercises, the positioning of the right hand and its interaction with the left hand must *never* be excluded from consideration.

Each portion of the scale or chord represented in the short kinesthetic exercises has unique characteristics, that is, focus points that are necessary points of emphasis that facilitate the smooth accurate execution of the sequence. Each exercise should be played **slowly** enough to allow the student to experience the feeling of executing each unique aspect correctly. In order to find and memorize these unique characteristics, the student must focus attention on the sequence of finger movements that produces each sequence of notes in the exercise. The student should also focus attention on the kinesthetic effects that result from the shifting accents produced by each of the 4 different articulation patterns. Pay close attention to the way in which the shifting focus points facilitate the execution of each kinesthetic exercise.
Remember, *slow, **Mindful*** practice is the key to successful technique.

Correct positioning of the hands and fingers is a necessary prerequisite for the successful use of any series of studies. Correct positioning for any given student will be determined by, among other things, the size and anatomy of the student's hands as well as by the teacher's preference concerning what is correct. In any case, the hands should be positioned so as to facilitate the execution of the exercises with as little *relaxed* motion as possible and with as little distance between the fingers and the keys and rings as possible. Smooth, precise fingering should flow effortlessly from a natural, relaxed hand position. Finally, practice sessions should be spaced in order to prevent repetitive stress.

There are many sources of information concerning the acquisition of proper hand position. Furthermore, individual teachers will have their own methods and exercises for developing and altering hand positions. The series of short exercises that follow are intended to help the student develop the capacity to play with as little motion and distance from the clarinet as possible. They are best used only with the guidance of an experienced teacher.

Exercise 1 is designed to position the right hand by establishing the shading point, i.e., the point at which the position of the right hand alters the pich of C. Gently resting the little finger of the right hand on either key #3 or #4 (F or Ab) will provide a balance point during the following exercises.

Ex.1. While playing middle C, gently place the fingers of the *right* hand in contact with the rings.
Slowly lift the fingers of the right hand to the closest point at which the pitch of C is no longer altered, thereby establishing the closest point at which the fingers of the right hand can be positioned. This should provide a stable resting position for the right hand. Once this position has been established, slowly play exercises 2 ,3 & 4. Be careful to maintain the position of the right hand while *slowly* playing the exercises with as little distance and motion in the left hand as possible. Be careful that once each finger of the left has been lifted, that it remains in place at the closest point possible to it's ring or hole. Also, once each finger is lifted it should not be allowed to move sympathetically in response to the movement of the other fingers in the sequence.

Ex. 5 & 6: Place the fingers of the right hand gently in contact with the rings, with the little finger in place on key #3 (F/C). Gently place the middle and ring fingers of the left hand in contact with their ring and hole. Place the left index finger gently on the G# & A keys of the throat register and the left thumb and contact with the register key. The left little finger should be gently positioned on Key # 1(E/B). Exercises 5 and 6 should be executed smoothly and evenly while all fingers remain in contact with their respective rings and keys and with no sympathetic finger movement.

Ex. 7 & 8: Exercise 7 begins with both hands placed as they were at the beginning of exercise 5, which is where they *should* be at the completion of exercise 6! Exercise 7 should finish with the right hand in the resting position that was established in exercise one. Exercise 8 should end with the fingers of both hands at the closest resting position possible, balanced by the contact of the little fingers (right on Key 3; left on key 1).

Ex.9 & 10: Exercises 9 & 10 are *memory scales*. Memory scales should be played in one continuous motion from beginning to end without reference to time. Begining and ending positions for both hands should now be established, with fingers no more than 1/4 inch from the rings & holes balanced by the gentle placement of the little fingers.

Kinesthetic Exercises

Kinesthetic practice is the active effort to memorize the _movements_ necessary to play each sequence correctly, _and_ to remember exactly how those movements _feel_ when the sequence is executed smoothly and accurately. Kenesthetic exercises _must_ be practiced **slowley** until the sensation (i.e., the feeling) of smooth, accurate execution is MEMORIZED.

Note that some of the focus points that facilitate the smooth execution of a sequence may occur at places other than the normal accent points (for example, on a note _other than_ the first of 4). Some notes may not speak adequately unless emphasized, even though they are not located at primary accent points. Pay close attention to the way in which the focus points change in relation to the four articulation patterns. Remember, the goal is always the smooth, accurate execution of each exercise.

The short kinesthetic exercises in each series are written out for reference only. Each exercise should be repeated until the movement becomes the focus and attention without reference to the notes. They are logically sequenced and should be easily memorized.

Series # 1

In order to _**temporally**_ isolate and exercise the left hand, the exercises in series #1 can be _practiced_ with the right hand rings & holes closed.

Series # 2

Some of the exercises (*) in series #2 can also be practiced with the right hand rings/holes closed.

4

6

Ibid

Practice in 1/2 steps to G#4, continuing to G# 5, *only* after mastering the Chromatic Altissmo studies.

Note fingering suggestions for the following two sequences:

etc.,

etc.,

Series #8

Chromatic Altissimo Exercises

Series #1

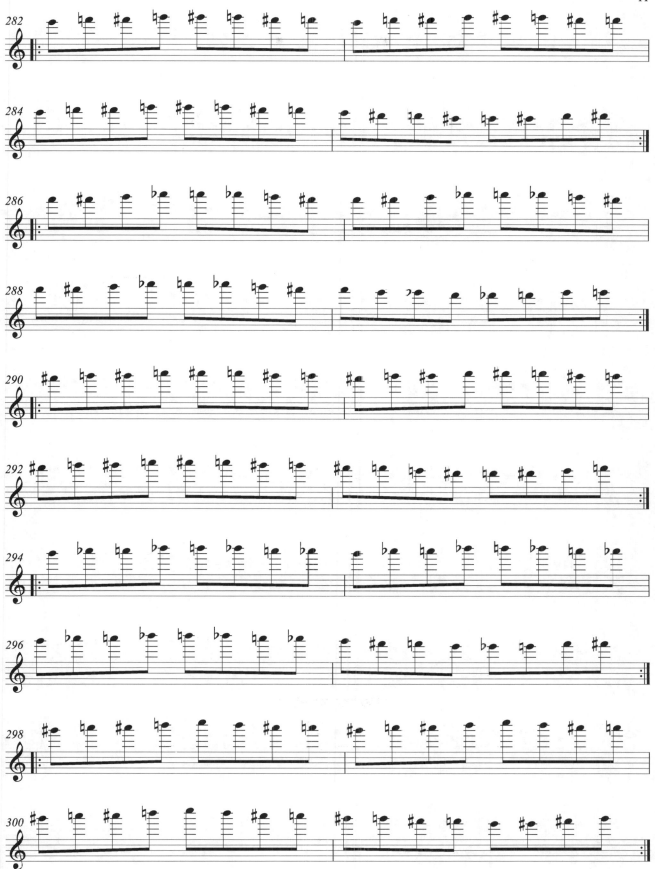

11

Chromatic Altissimo Exercises

Series #2

Series #3

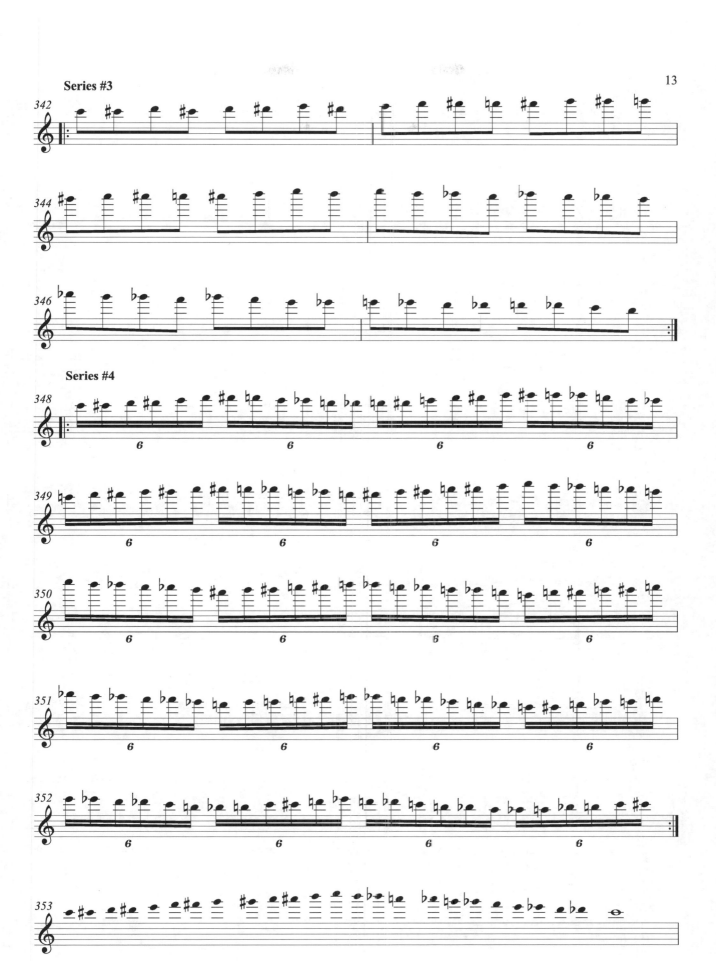

Series #4

Supplemental Chromatic Exercises

15

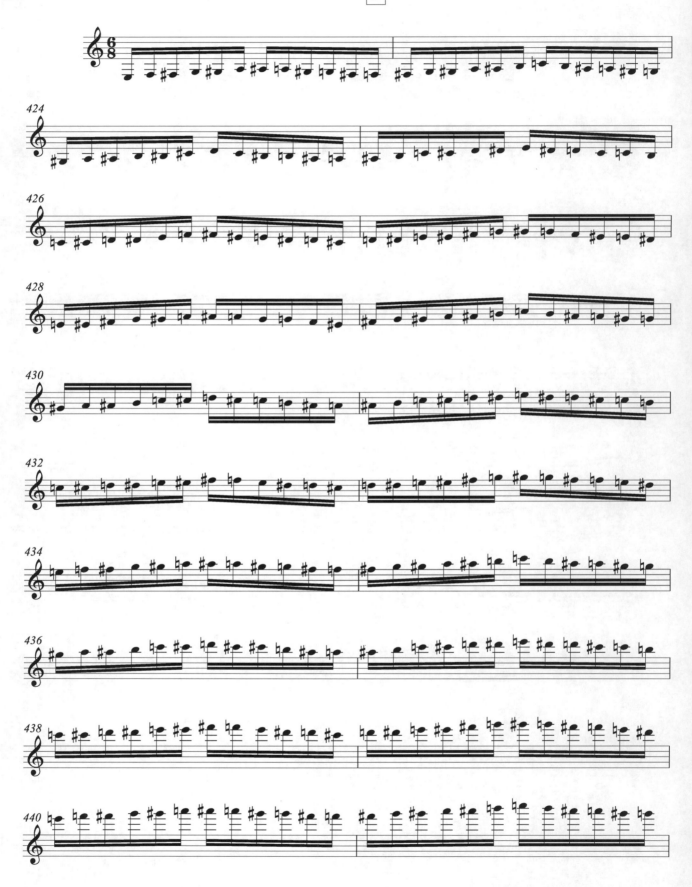

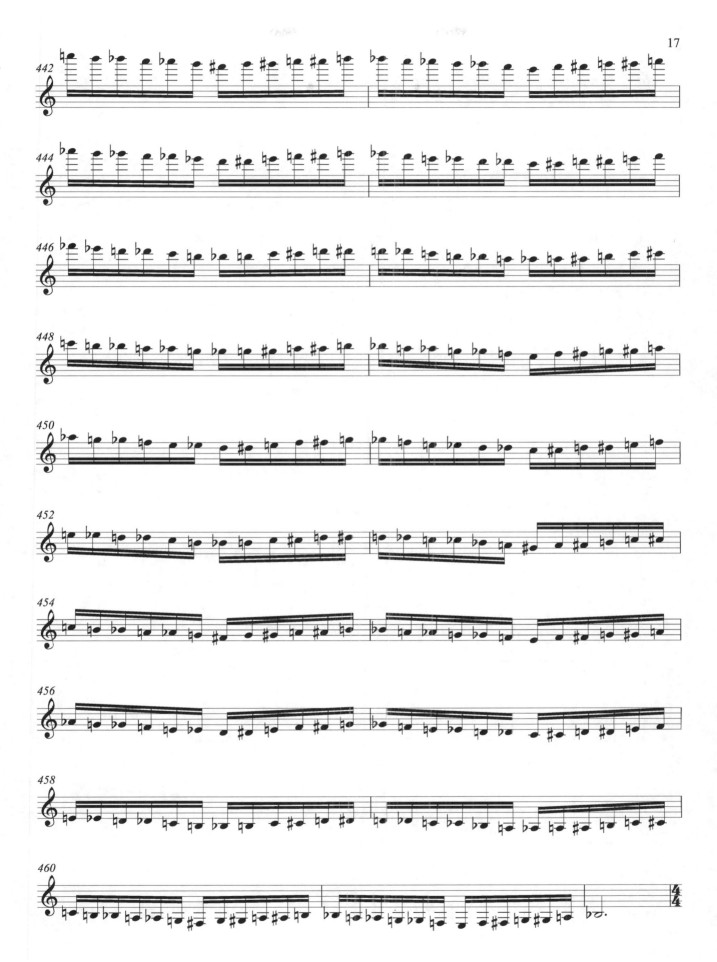

4

Major & Minor Scale Studies For The Left Hand

Kinesthetic Memory Exercises

Kinesthetic Memory Exercises

A   Harmonic Minor

Scale study(read)

519 Db Major

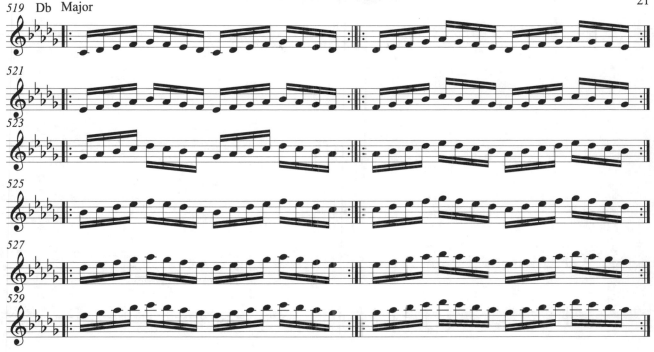

Scale study (read)

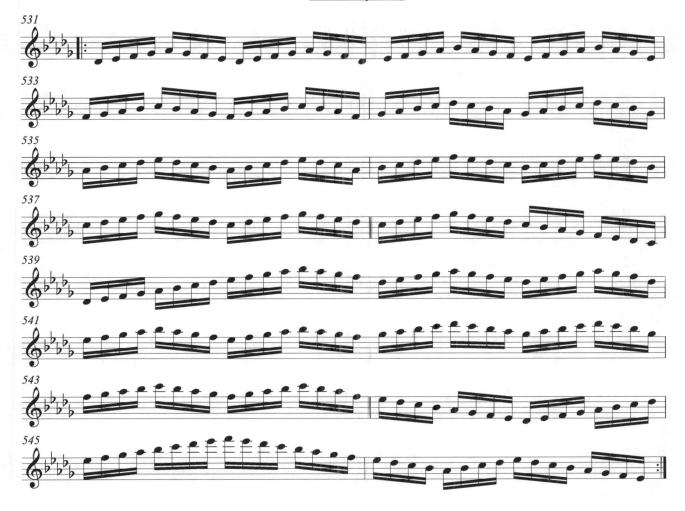

Kinesthetic Memory Exercises

Bb Harmonic Minor

Scale study(read)

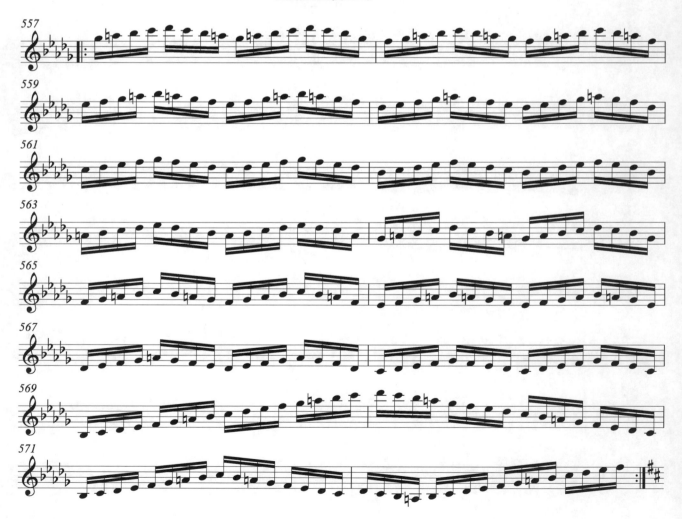

Kinesthetic Memory Exercises

573   D Major

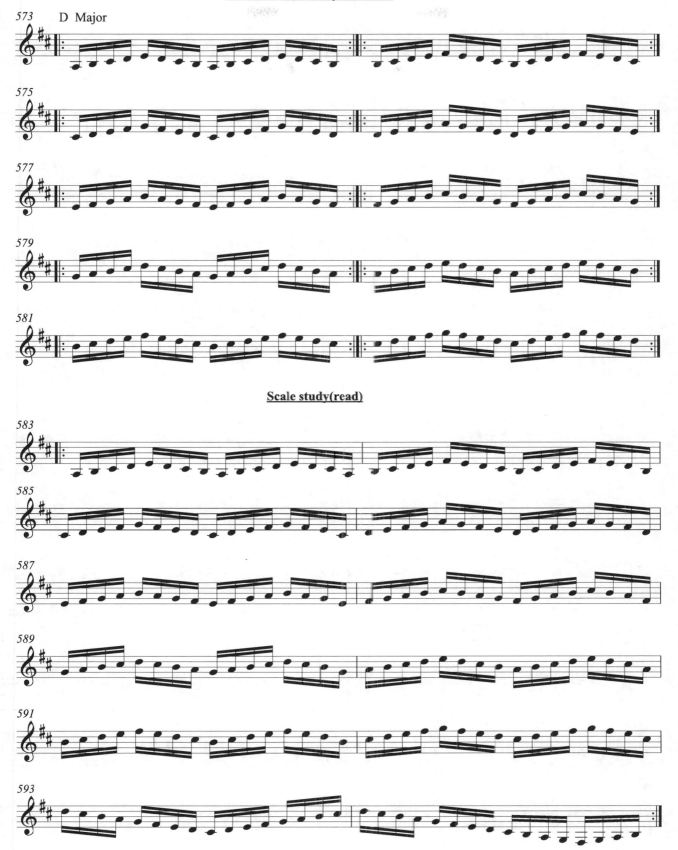

Scale study(read)

24

Kinesthetic Memory Exercises

B   Harmonic Minor

Scale study(read)

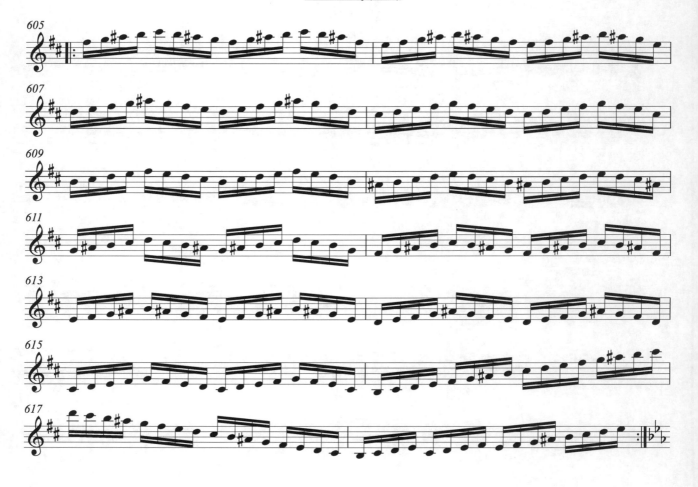

Kinesthetic Memory Exercises

Eb Major

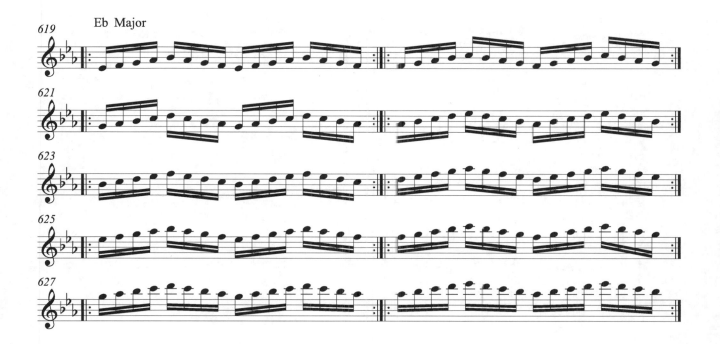

Scale study(read)

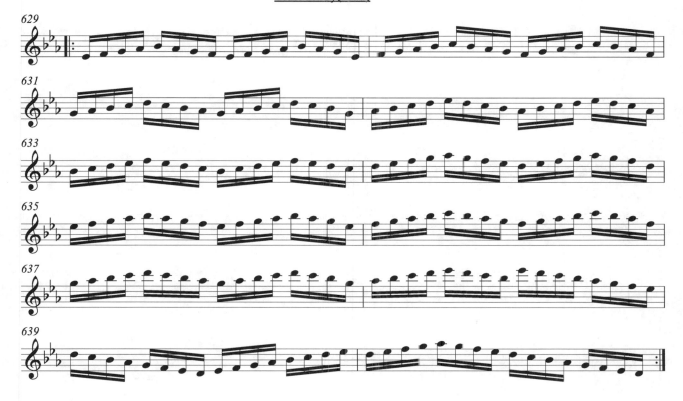

Kinesthetic Memory Exercises

C Harmonic Minor

Scale study(read)

Kinesthetic Memory Exercises

E Major

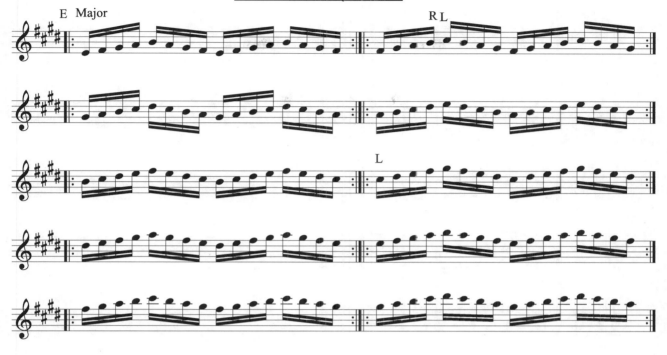

Scale study(read)

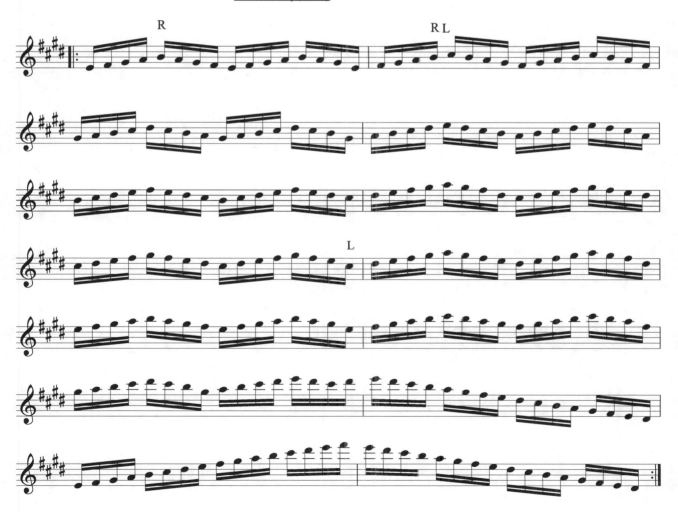

Kinesthetic Memory Exercises

C# Harmonic Minor

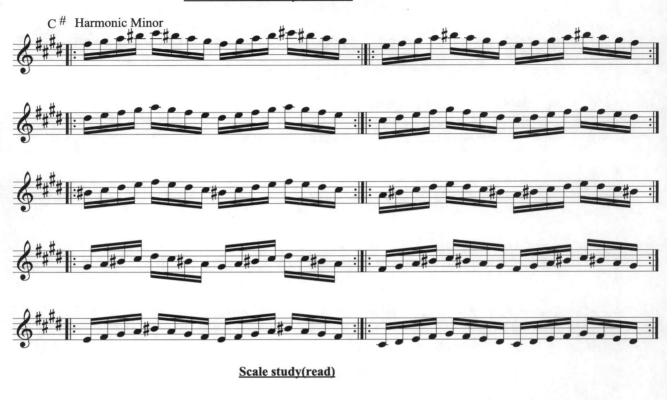

Scale study(read)

Kinesthetic Memory Exercises

F   Major

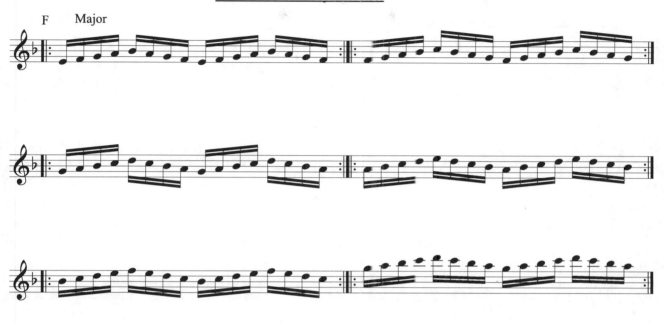

Scale study(read)

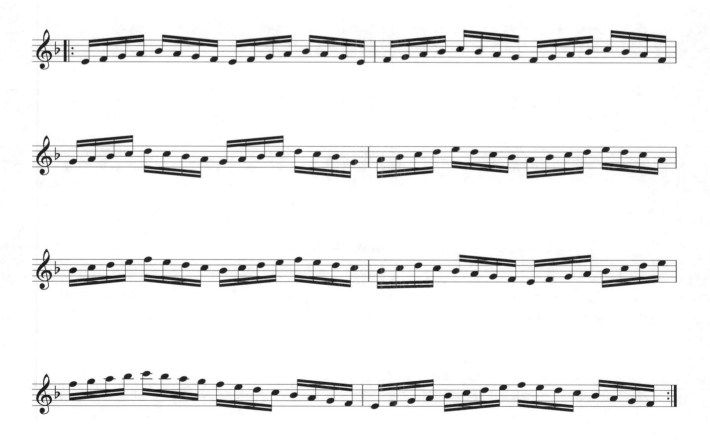

Kinesthetic Memory Exercises

D   Harmonic Minor

Scale study(read)

Kinesthetic Memory Exercises

F# Major

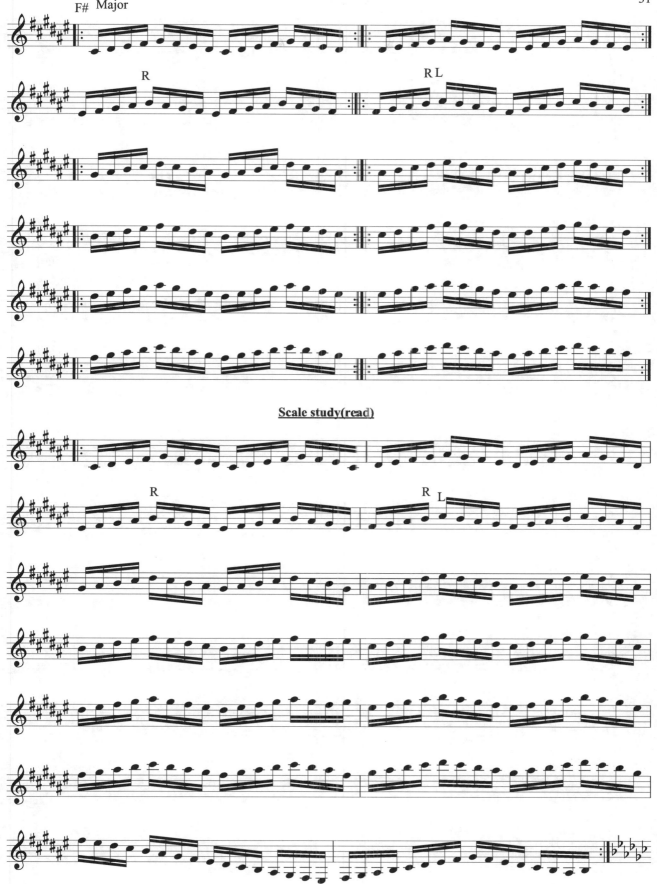

Scale study(read)

Kinesthetic Memory Exercises

E b   Harmonic Minor

Scale study(read)

Kinesthetic Memory Exercises

G   Major

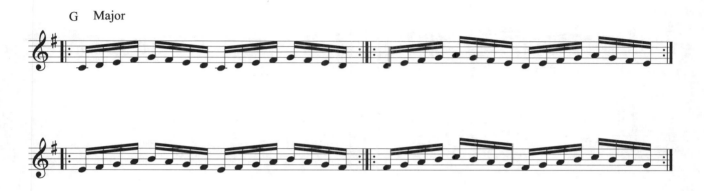

Scale study(read)

Kinesthetic Memory Exercises

E   Harmonic Minor

Scale study(read)

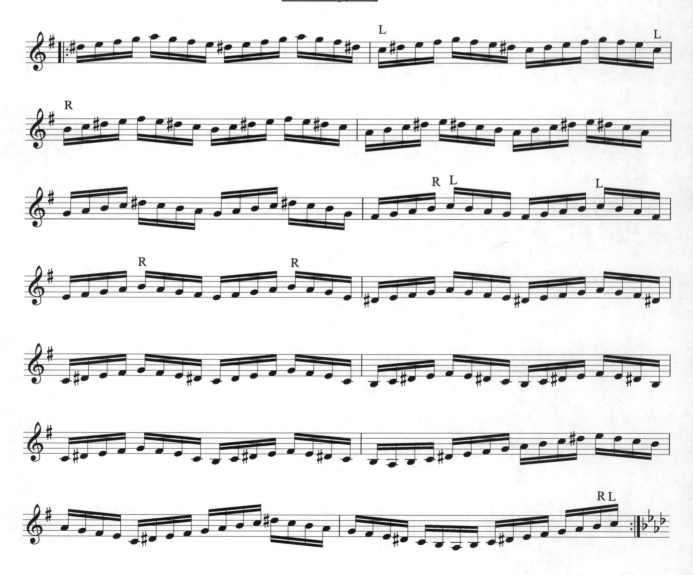

Kinesthetic Memory Exercises

Ab   Major

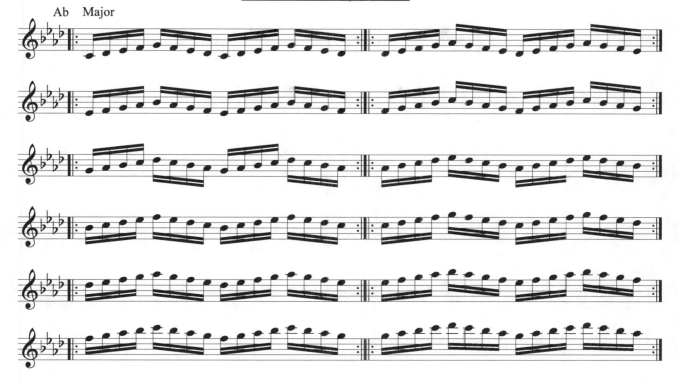

Scale study(read)

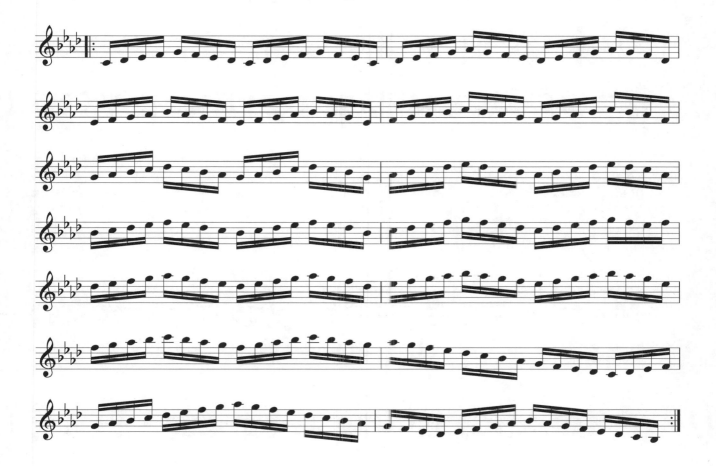

Kinesthetic Memory Exercises

Scale study(read`

F Harmonic Minor

38

Kinesthetic Memory Exercises

A Major

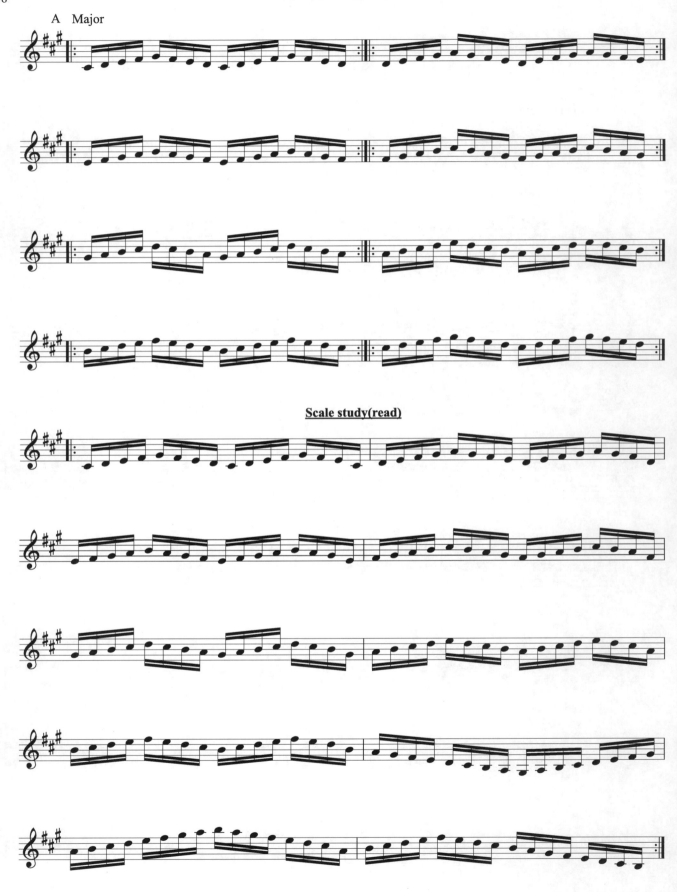

Scale study(read)

F#   Harmonic Minor

Scale study(read)

Kinesthetic Memory Exercises

Bb   Major

Scale study(read)

Kinesthetic Memory Exercises

G   Harmonic Minor

Scale study(read)

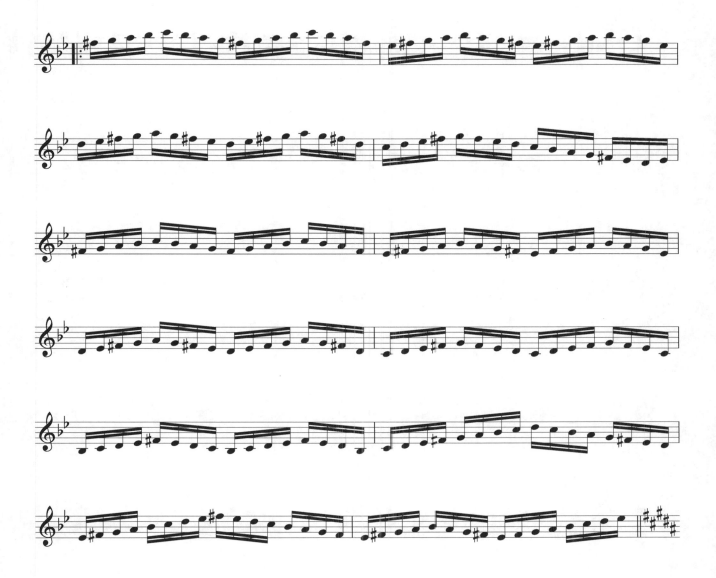

Kinesthetic Memory Exercises

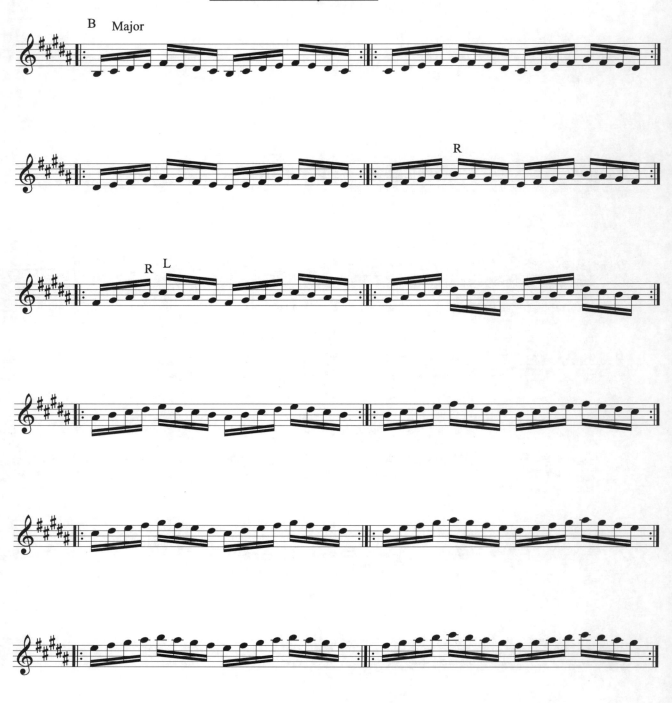

Scale study(read)

B Major

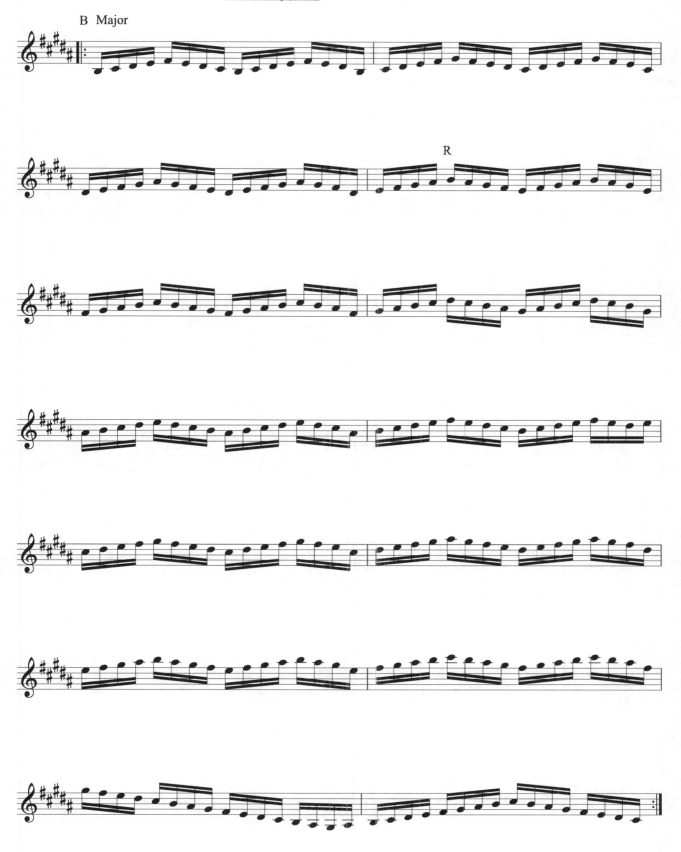

44

Kinesthetic Memory Exercises

G # Harmonic Minor

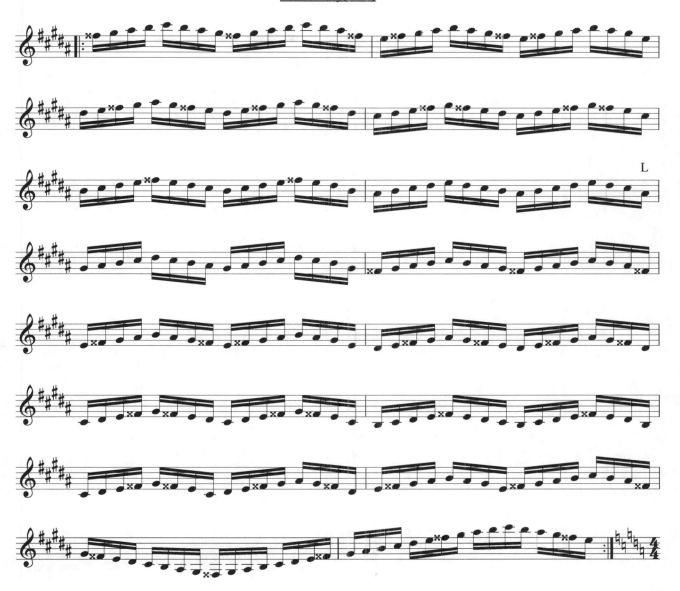

L

Diatonic, Chromatic & Chordal Exercises
For the Left Hand

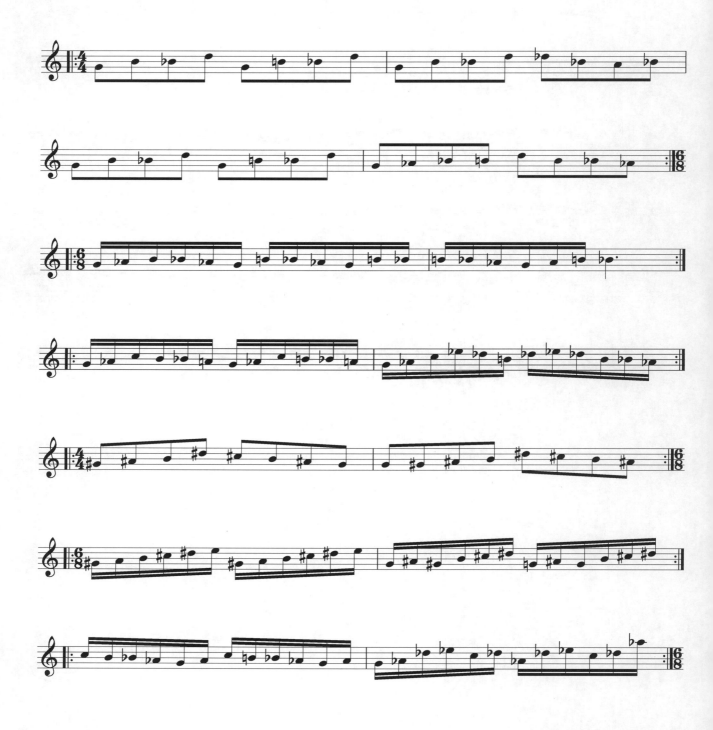

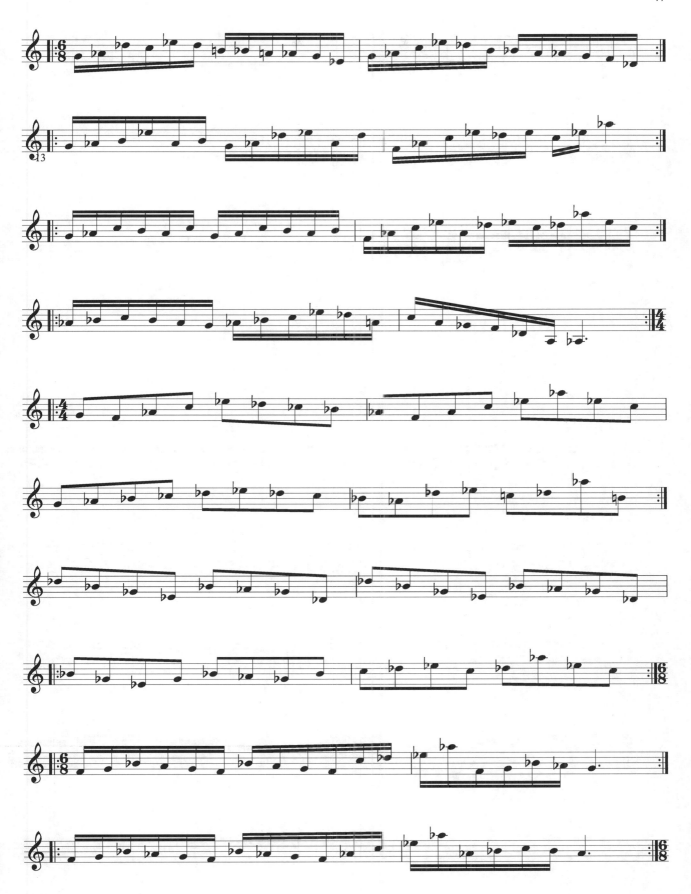

48

MAJOR SCALES

Each line is a set of **two** *Kinesthetic* exercises. The two short exercises that conmprise each set should be practiced *seprately* then played together as a single four measure Kinesthetic exercise. To facilitate memory, particularly in the altissimo, the secomd exercise in each set can be further devided into two one measure kinesthetic exercises. **Slow** practice is essential. After slow Kinesthetic practice, the eintire series of *memorized* Kinesthetic exercises can be played sequentially at increasing speeds. However, it should always be remembered that *slow* practice is the key to sucessful execution. The *memory scales (scales without stems)* should be executed in one smooth motion without effort or thought.

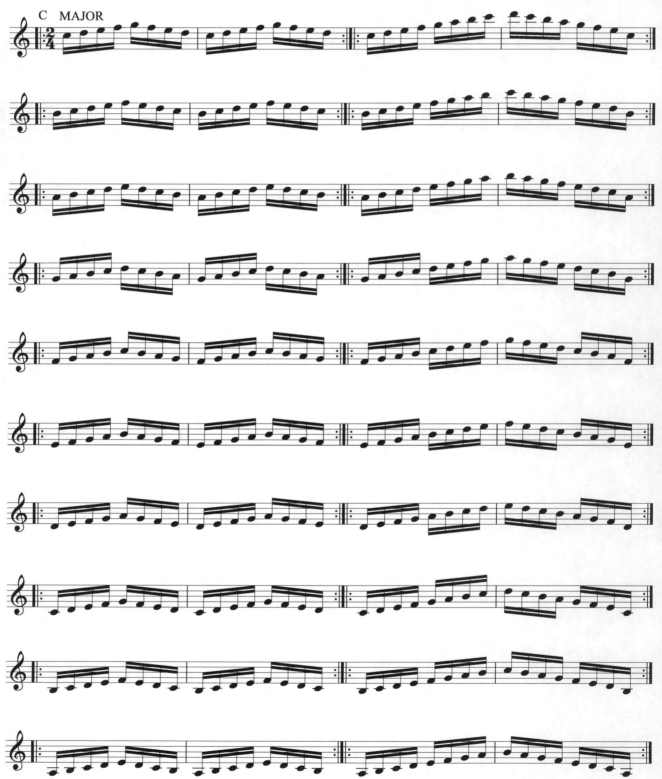

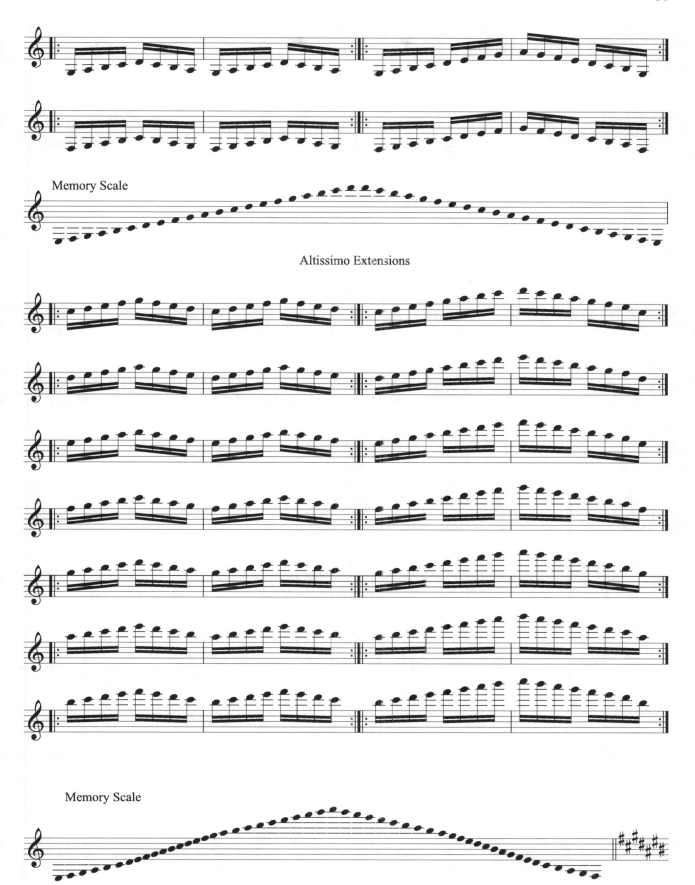

Memory Scale

Altissimo Extensions

Memory Scale

C # MAJOR

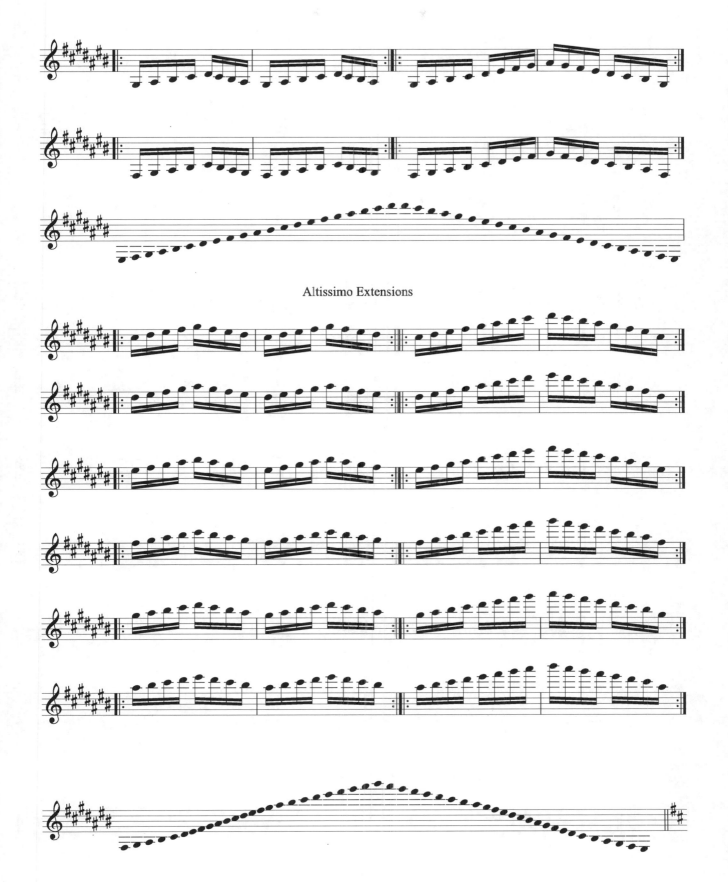

Altissimo Extensions

D MAJOR

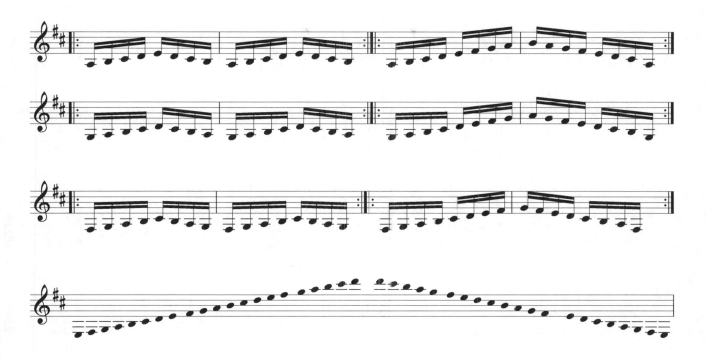

Altissimo Extensions

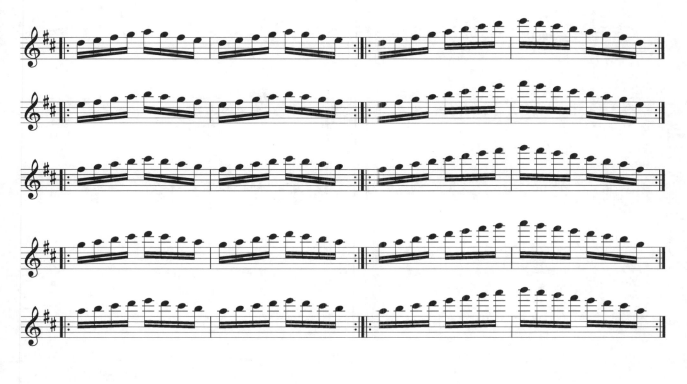

Eb MAJOR

Eb

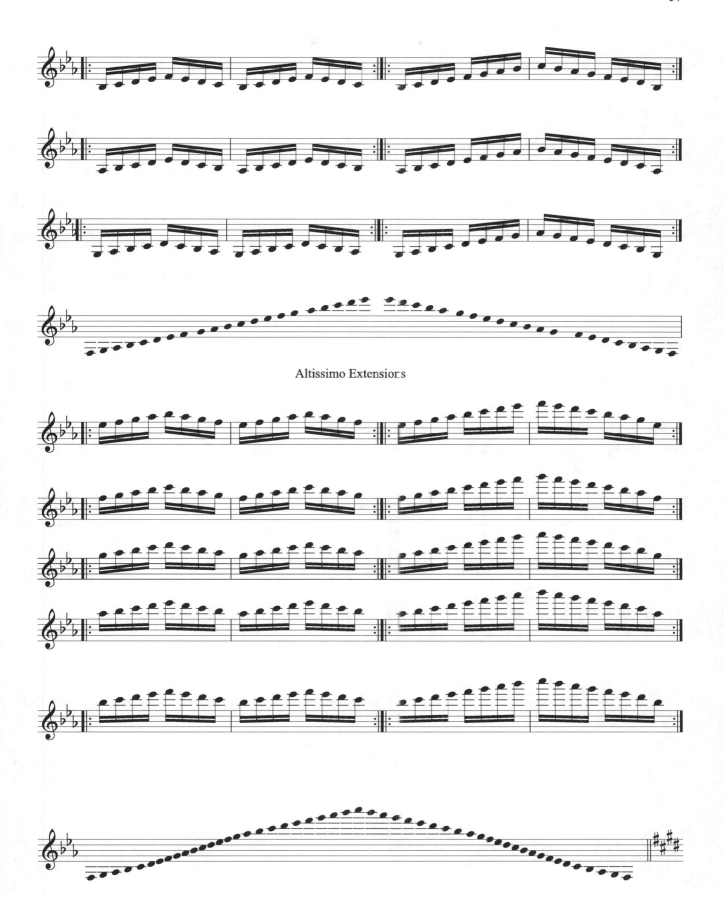

Altissimo Extensions

58

E MAJOR

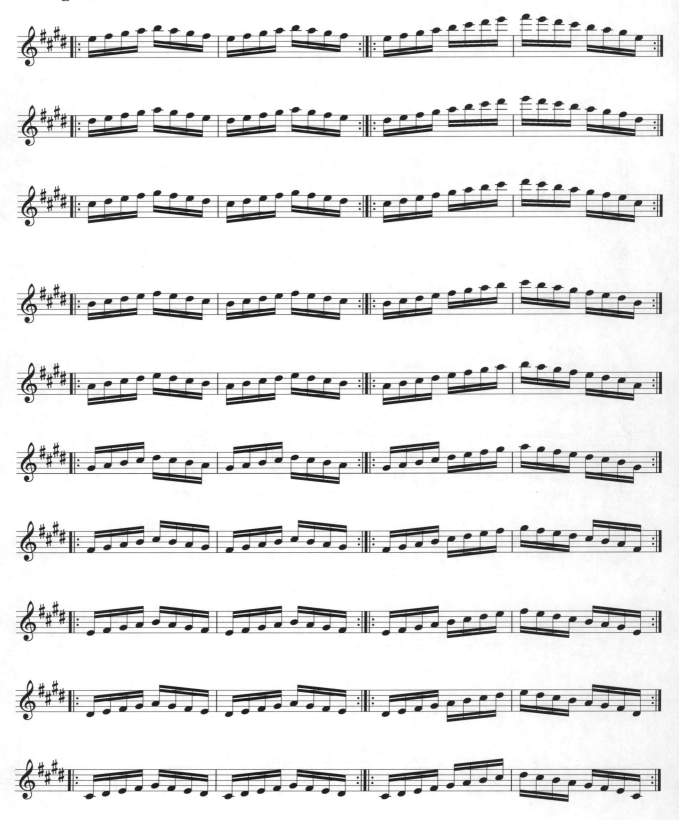

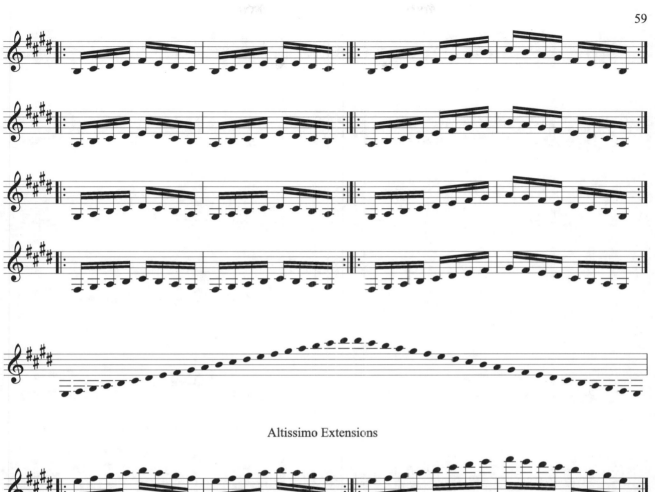

Altissimo Extensions

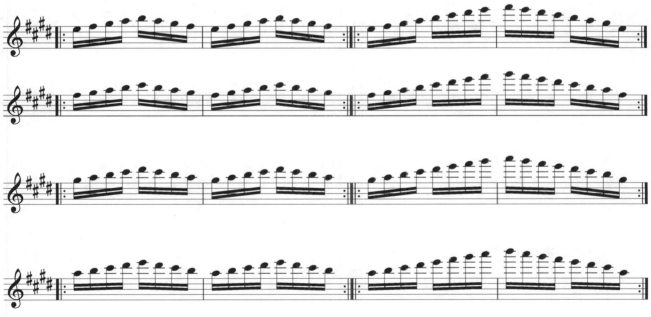

60

F MAJOR

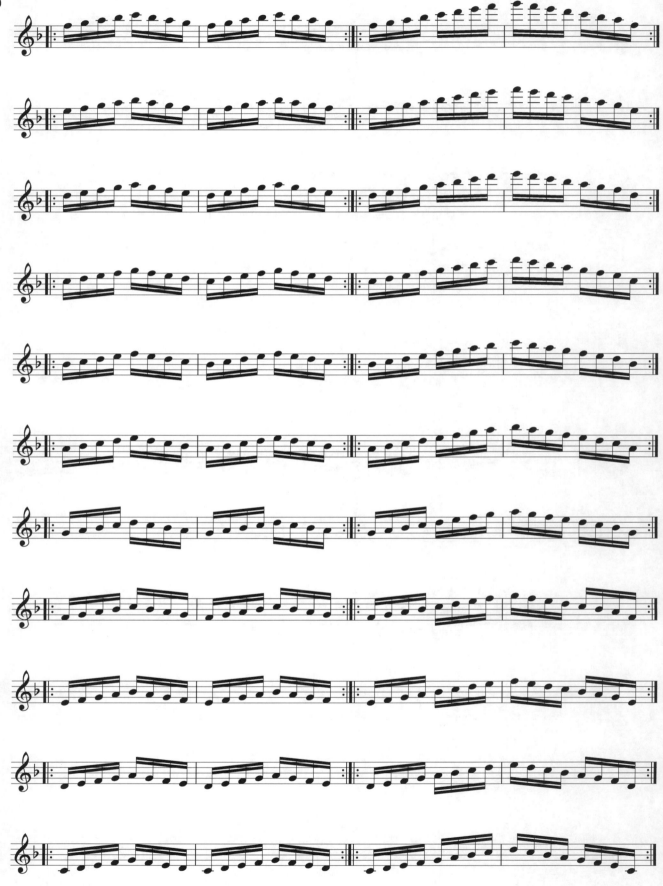

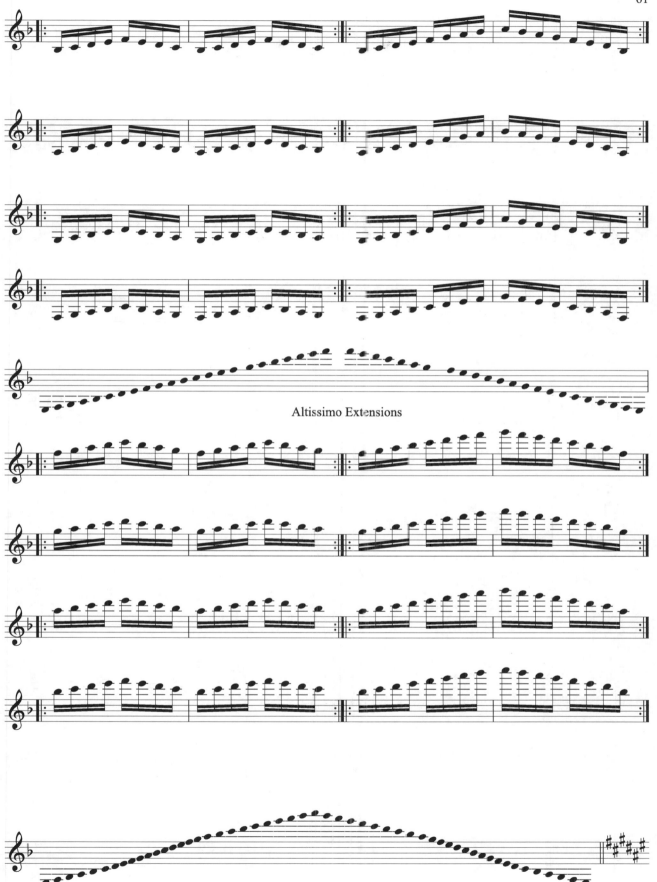

Altissimo Extensions

F[#] MAJOR

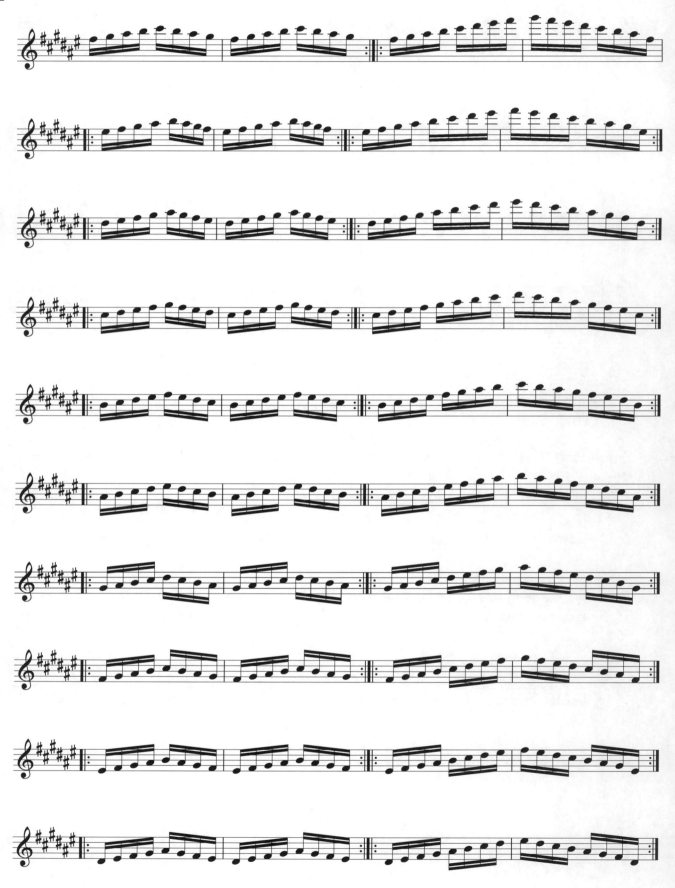

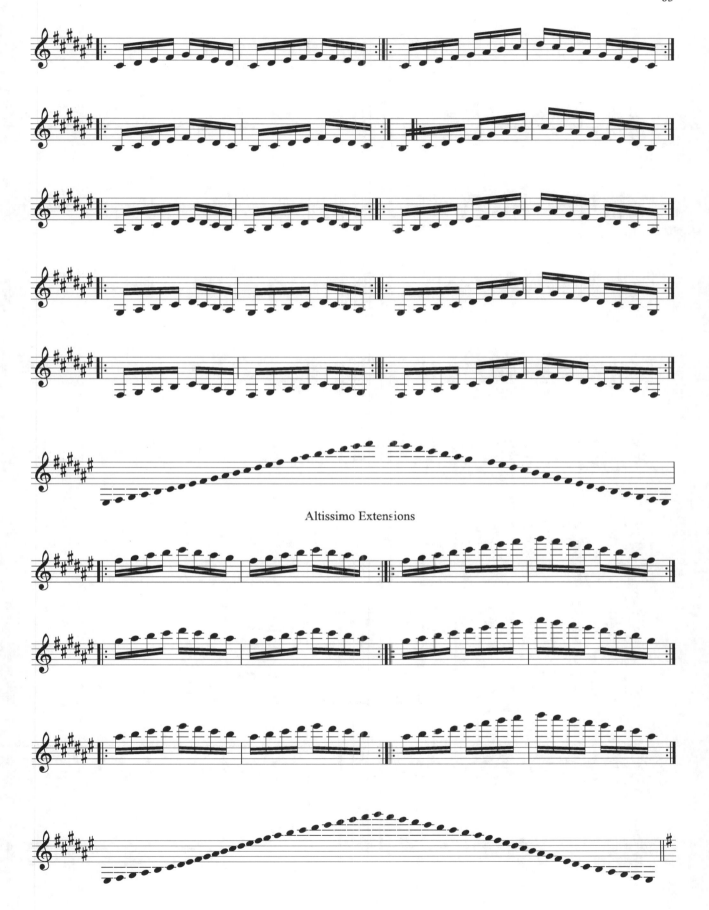

Altissimo Extensions

G MAJOR

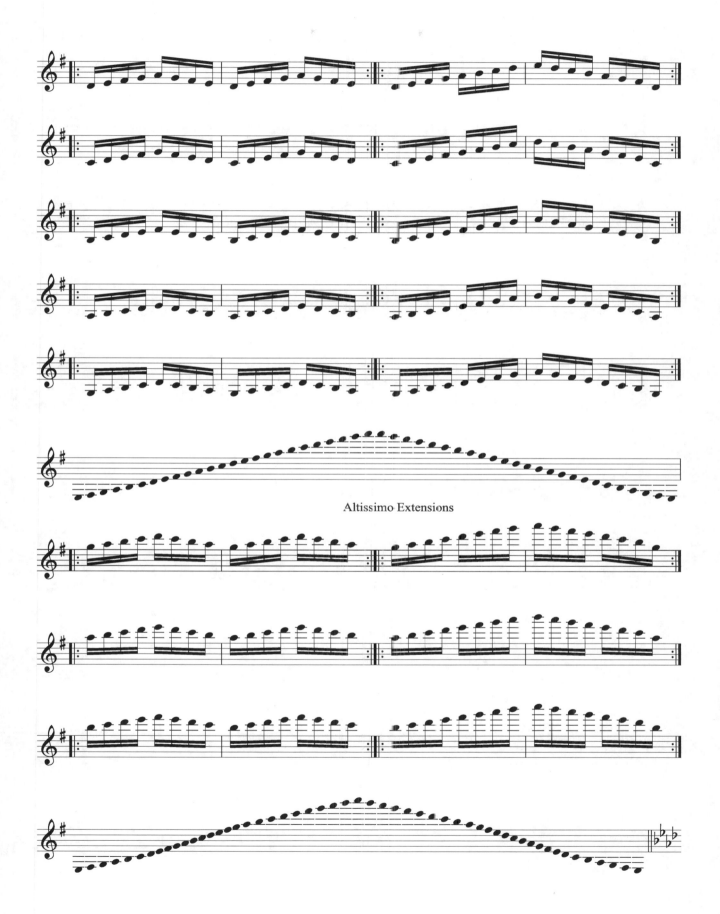

Altissimo Extensions

Ab MAJOR

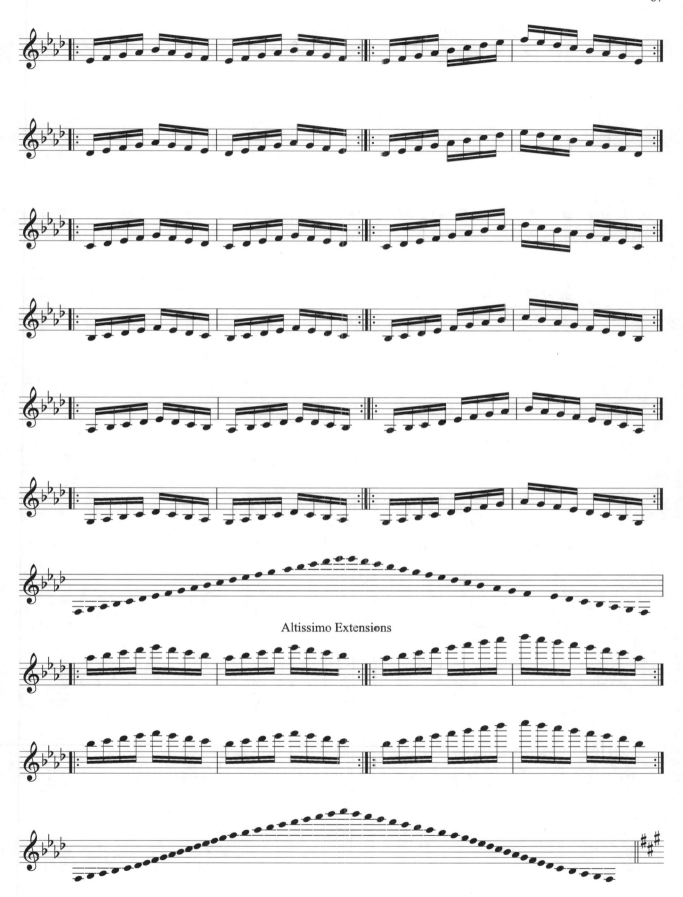

Altissimo Extensions

A MAJOR

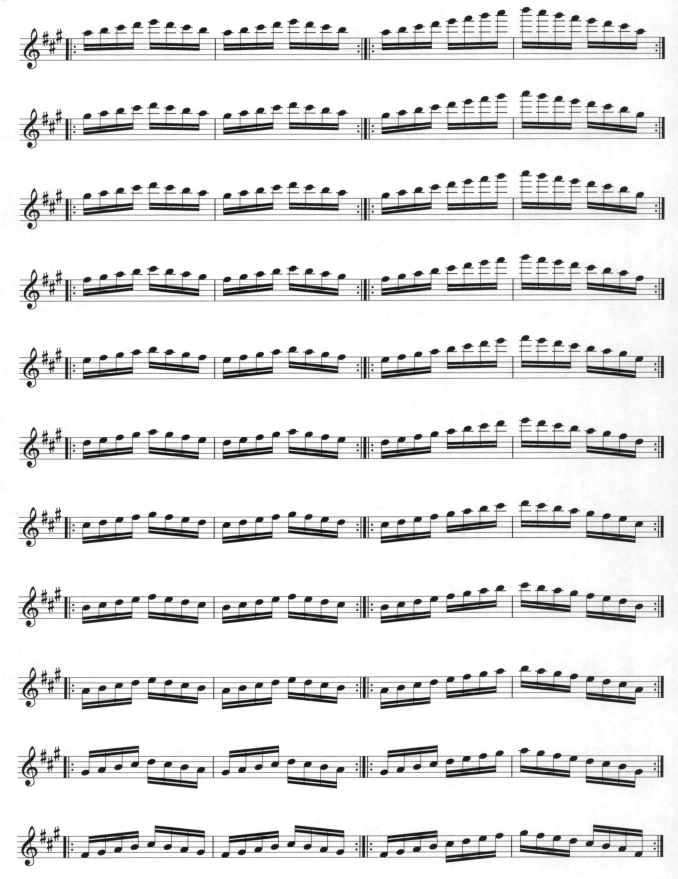

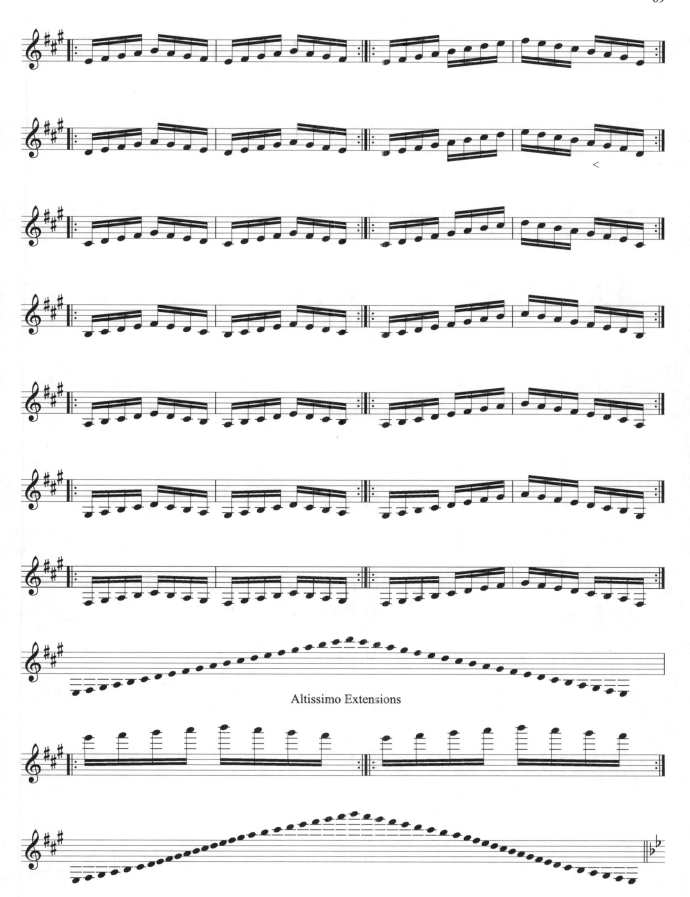

Altissimo Extensions

Bb MAJOR

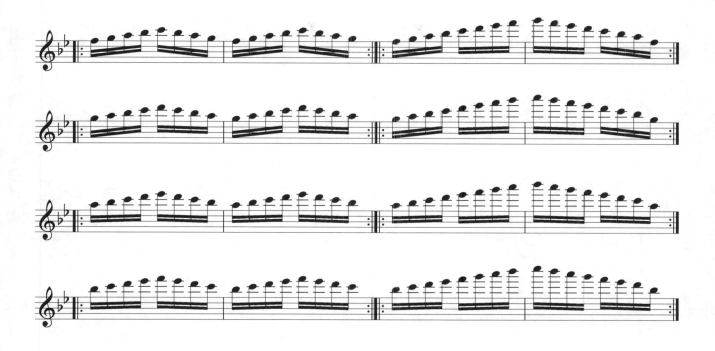

B MAJOR

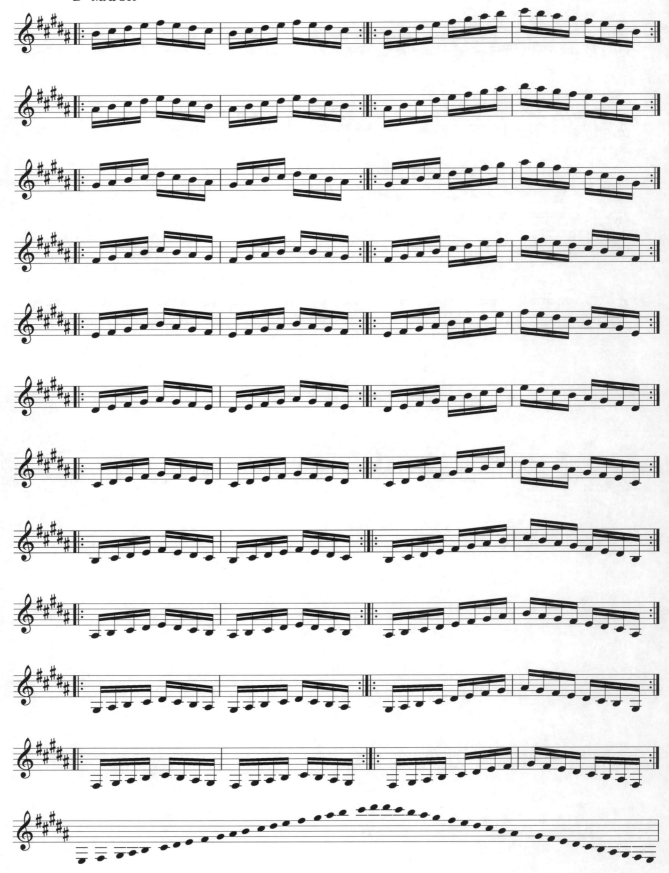

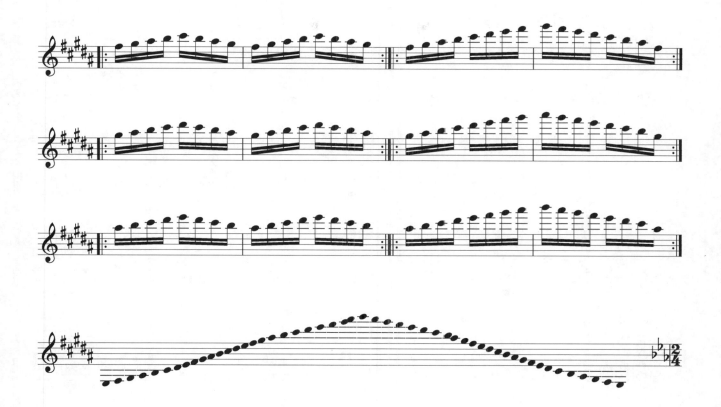

MINOR SCALE STUDIES

C Harmonic Minor

75

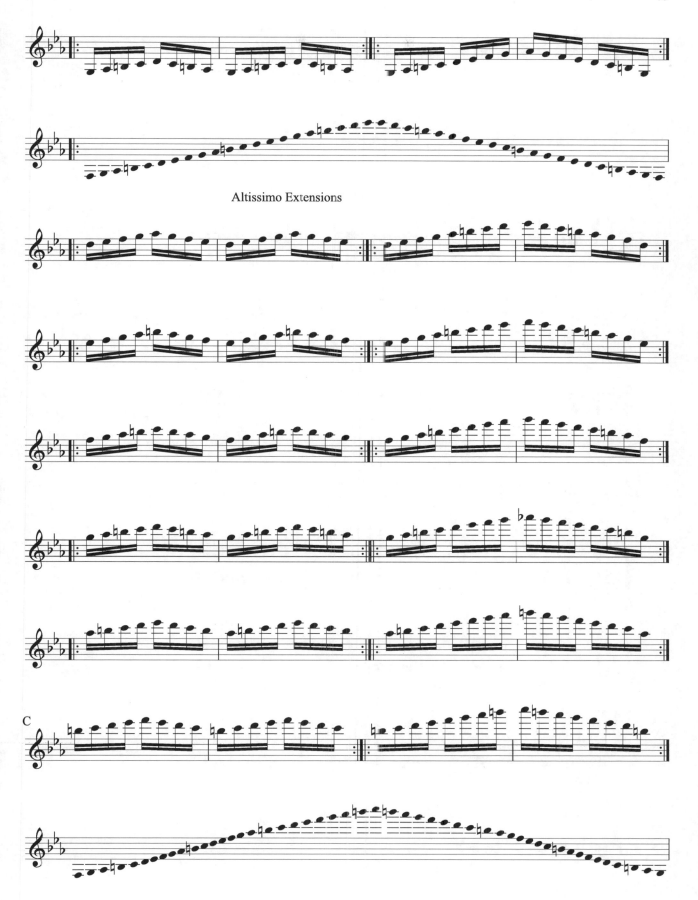

Altissimo Extensions

C Melodic Minor

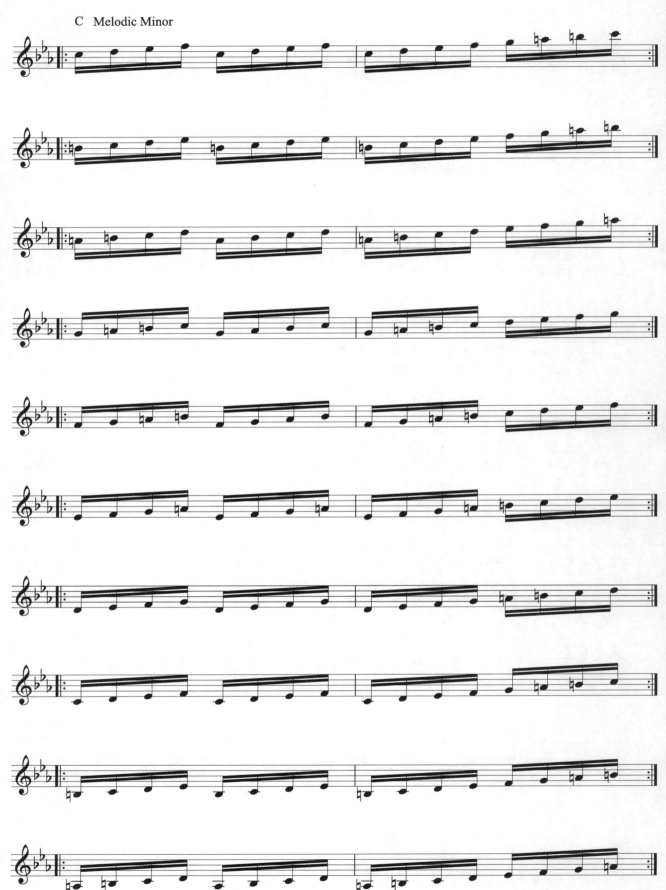

The Altissimo (*) portion of the memory scale is to be completed only after the final kinesthetic series and the review scale for each scale have been completed.

Final Kinesthetic series

Review scale

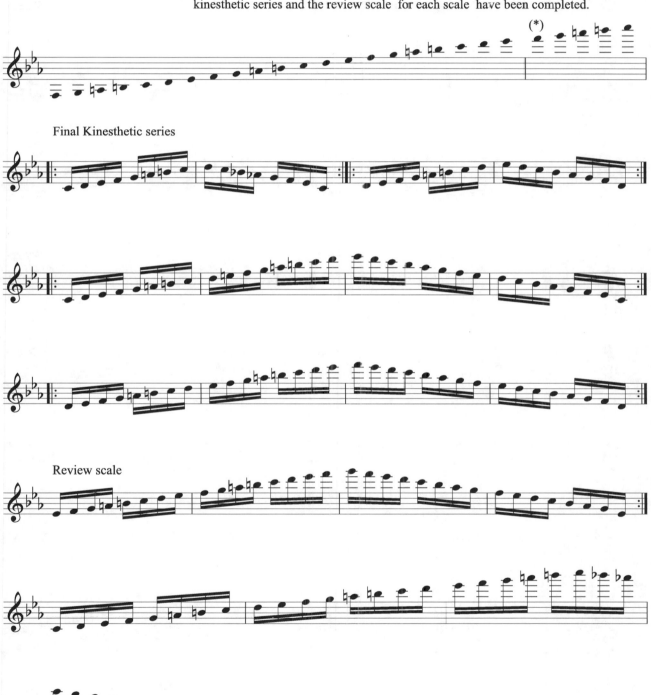

C# Harmonic Minor   C#

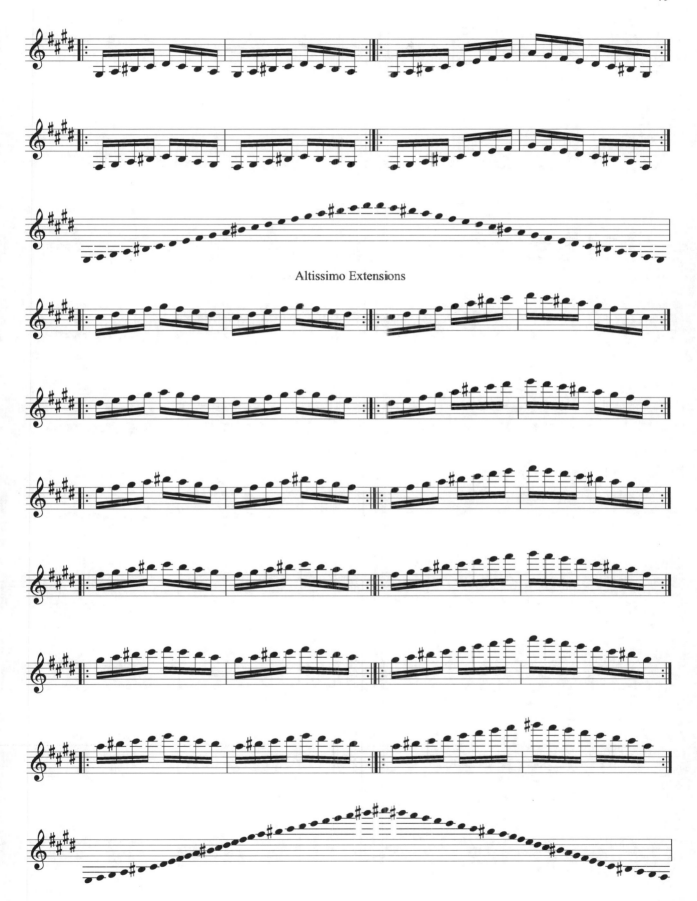

Altissimo Extensions

C#   Melodic Minor

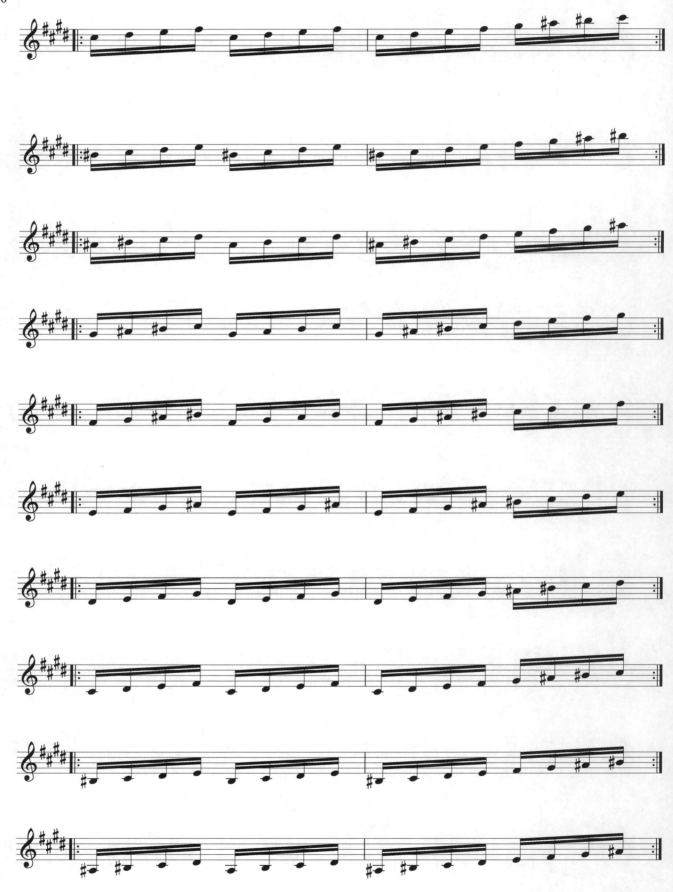

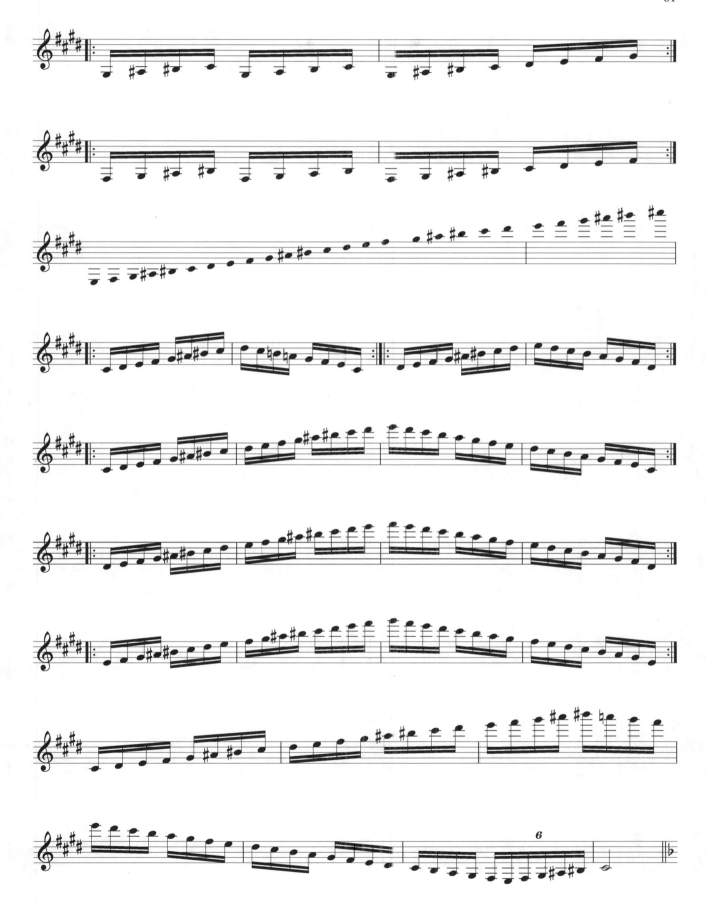

D   Harmonic Minor

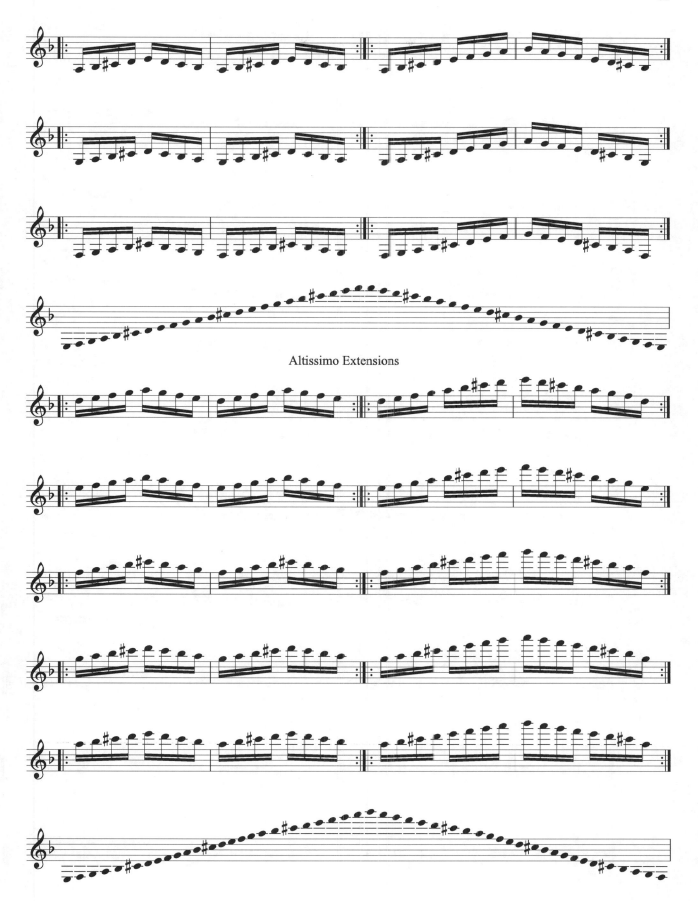

Altissimo Extensions

84   D   Melodic Minor

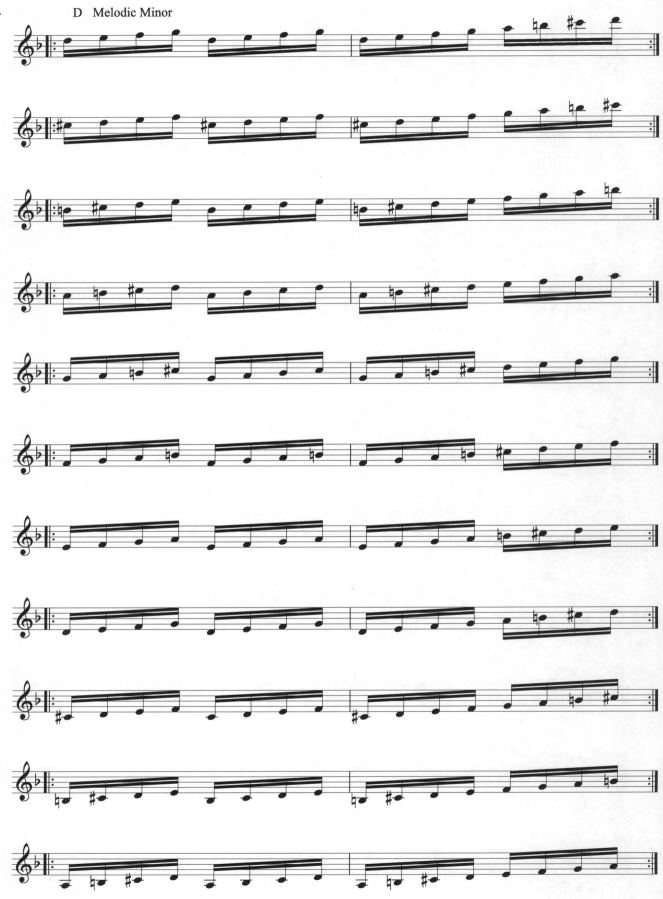

Eb   Harmonic Minor

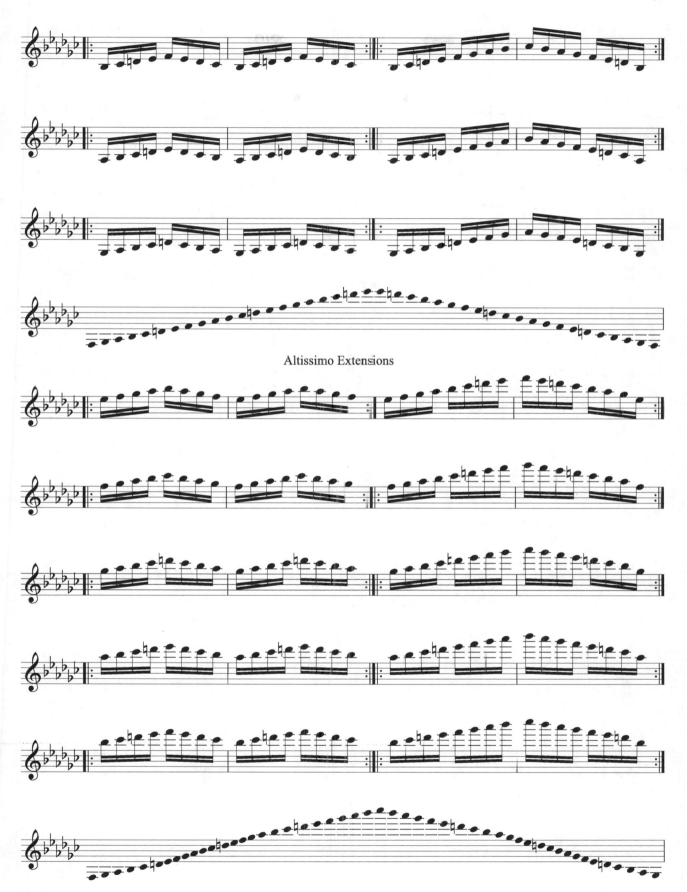

Altissimo Extensions

Eb   Melodic Minor

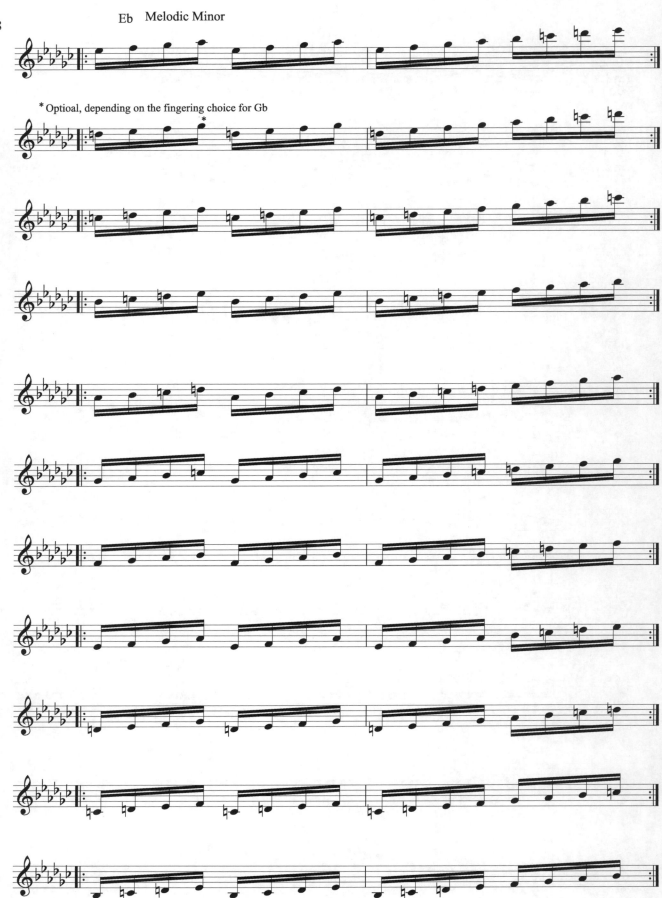

* Optioal, depending on the fingering choice for Gb

E   Harmonic Minor

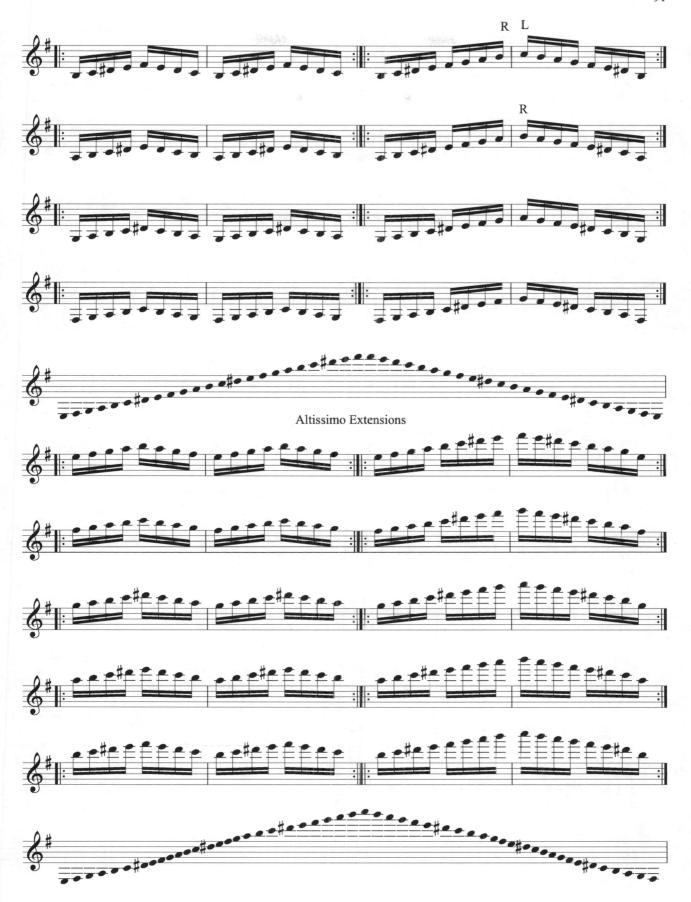

Altissimo Extensions

E Melodic Minor

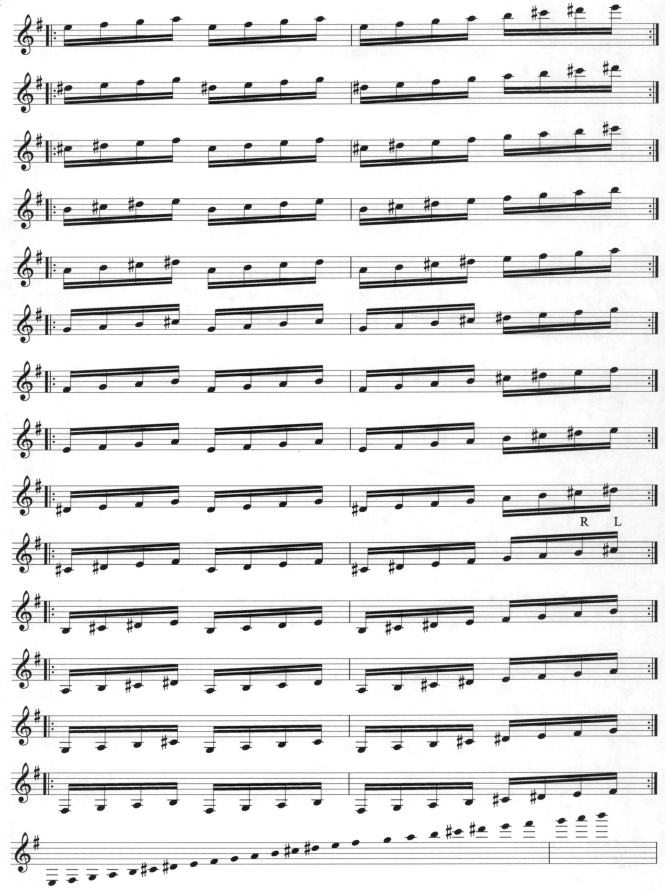

93

F   Harmonic Minor

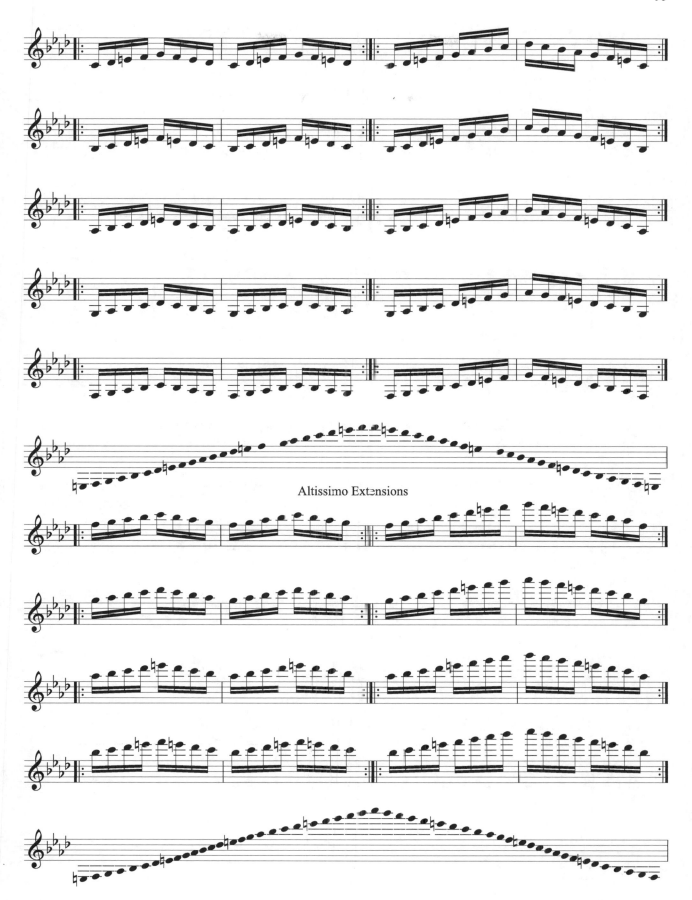

Altissimo Extensions

95

96 F Melodic Minor

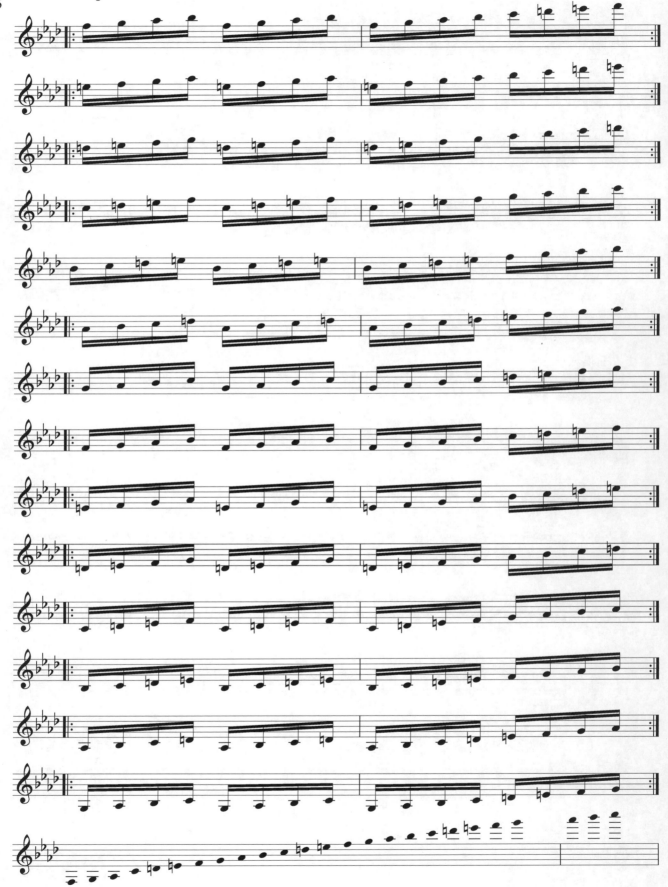

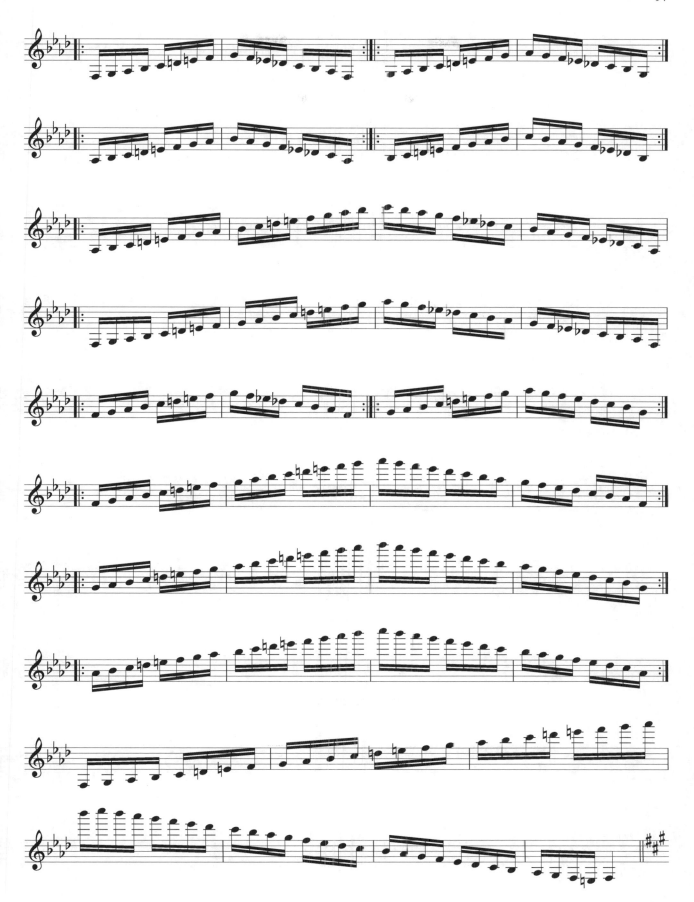

F#   Harmonic Minor

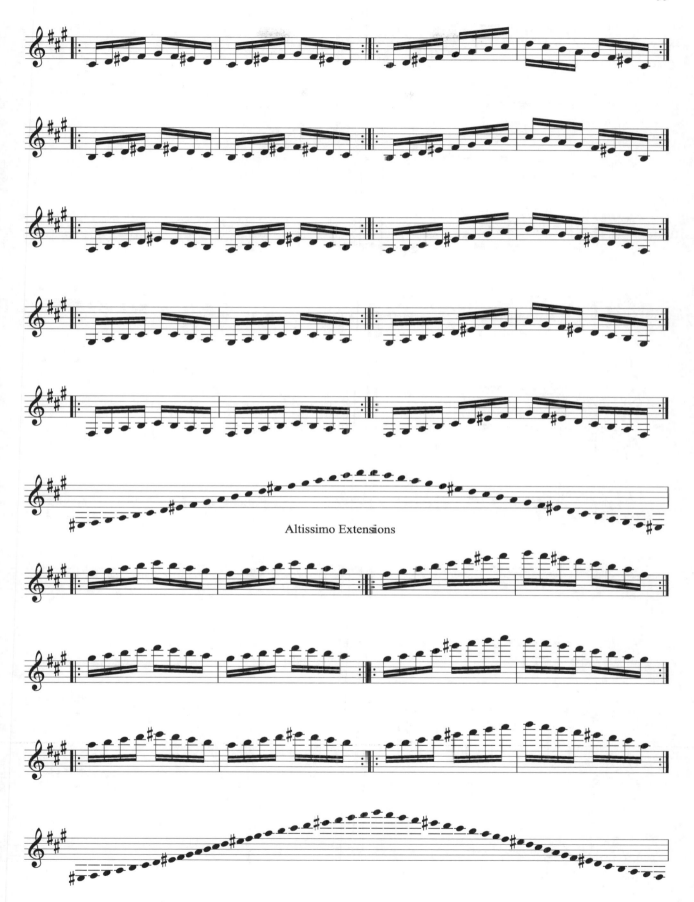

Altissimo Extensions

F#   Melodic Minor

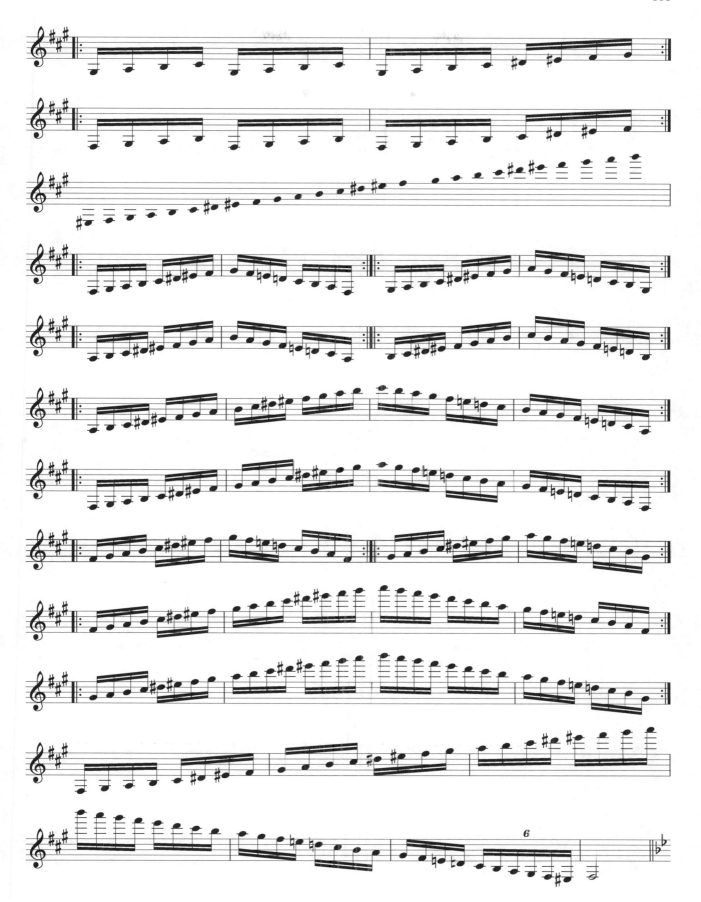

102   G   Harmonic Minor

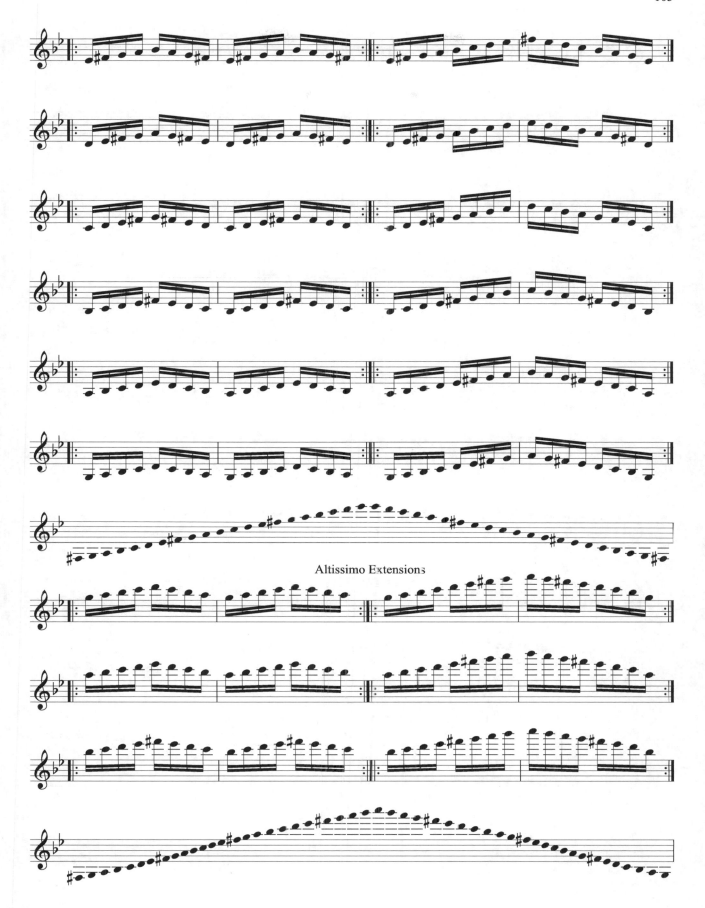

Altissimo Extensions

104

G   Melodic Minor

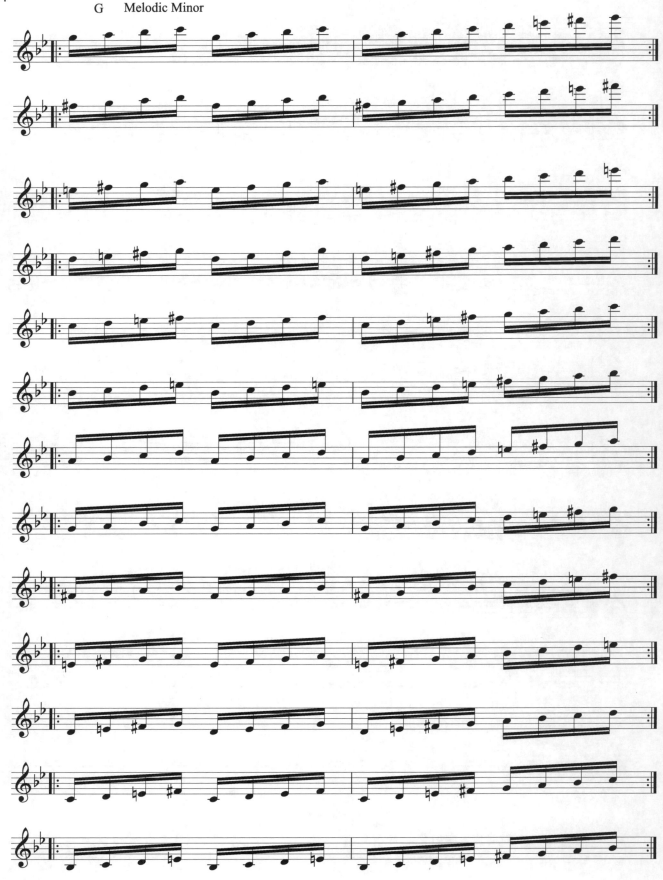

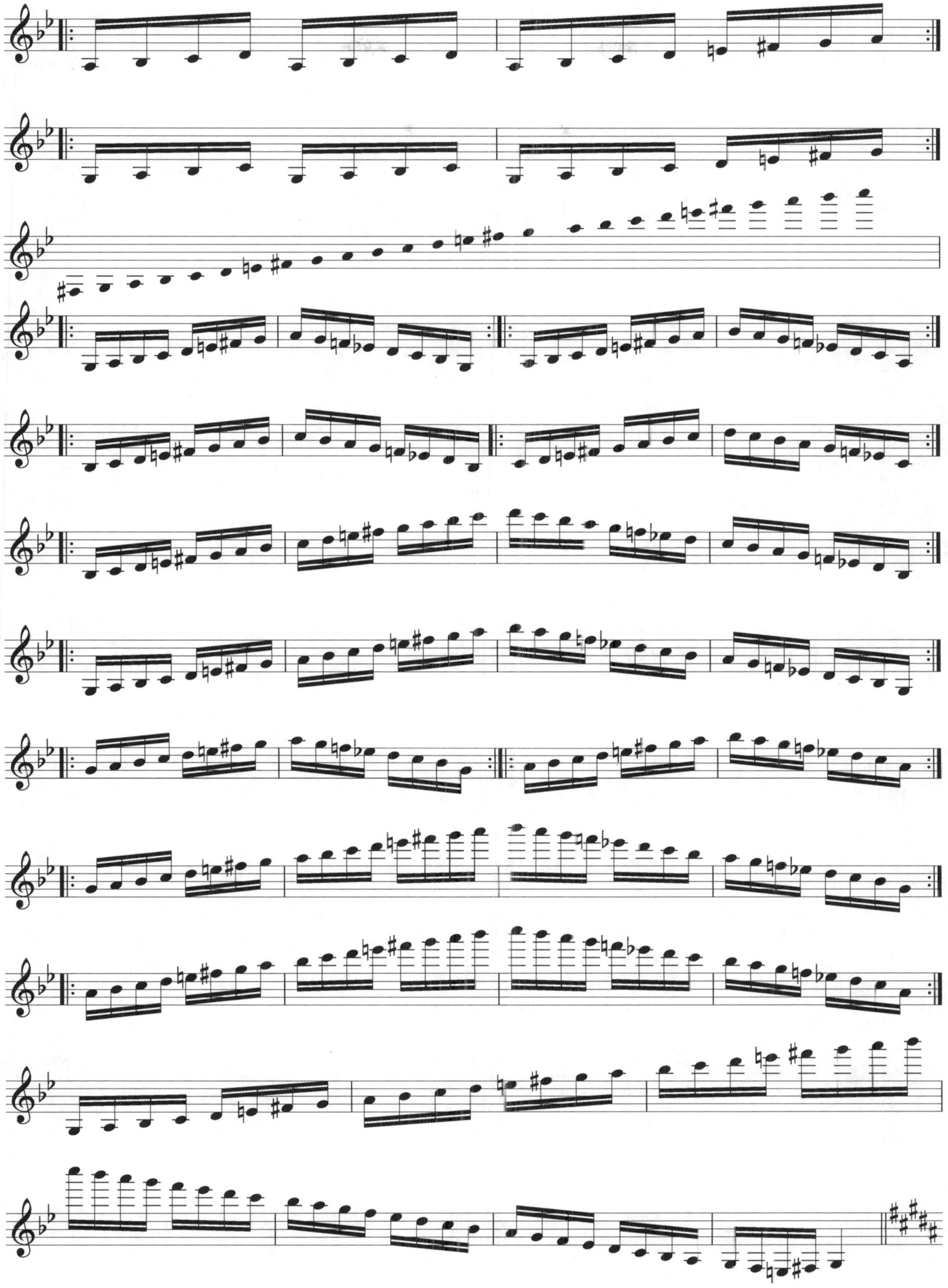

106

G# Harmonic Minor

107

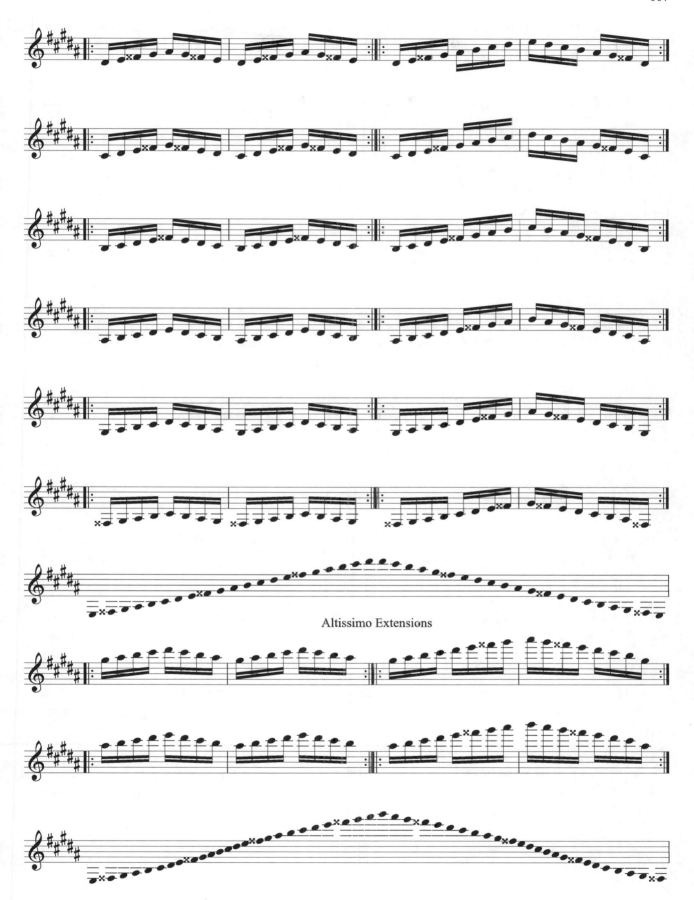

Altissimo Extensions

108   G# Melodic Minor

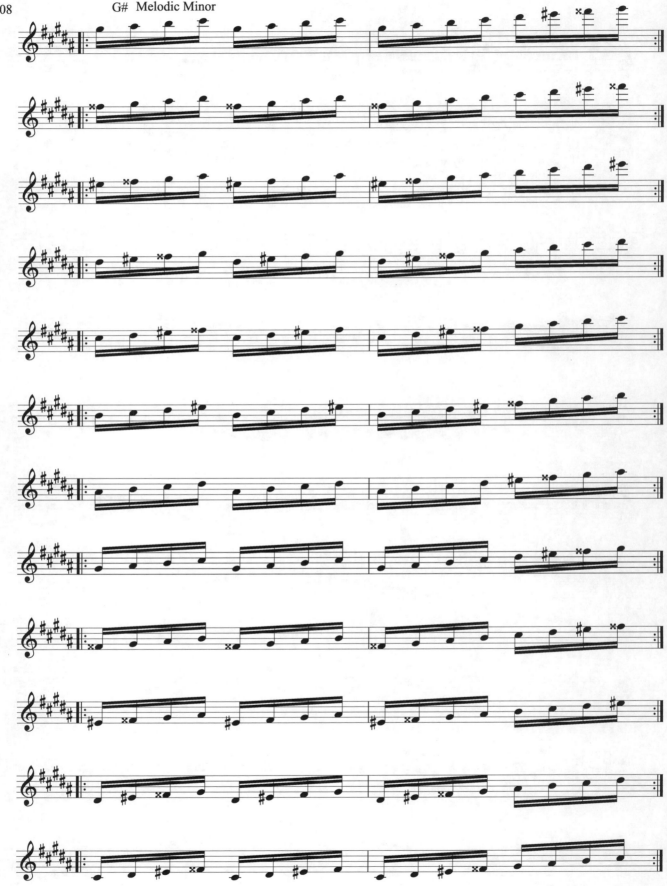

A   Harmonic Minor

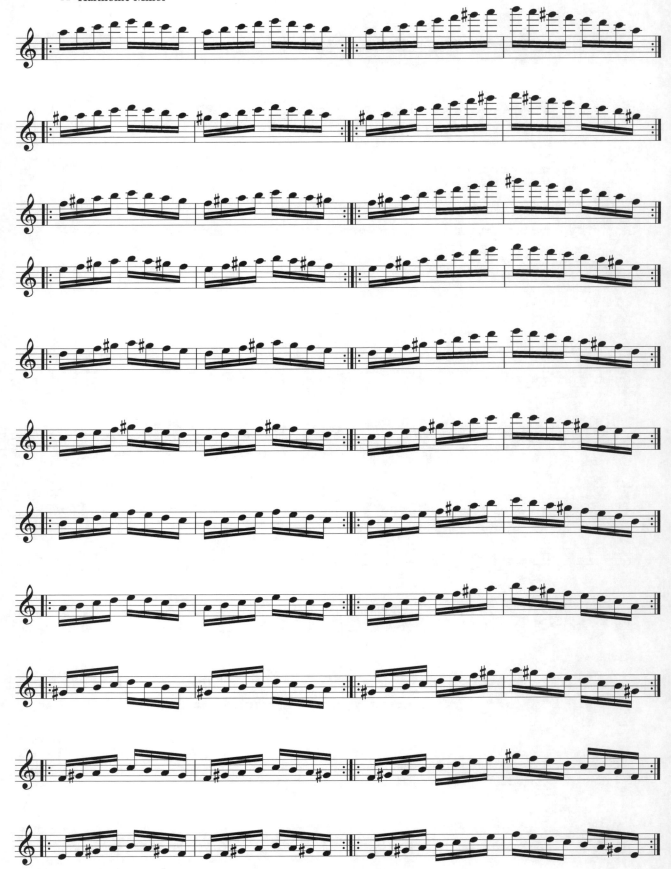

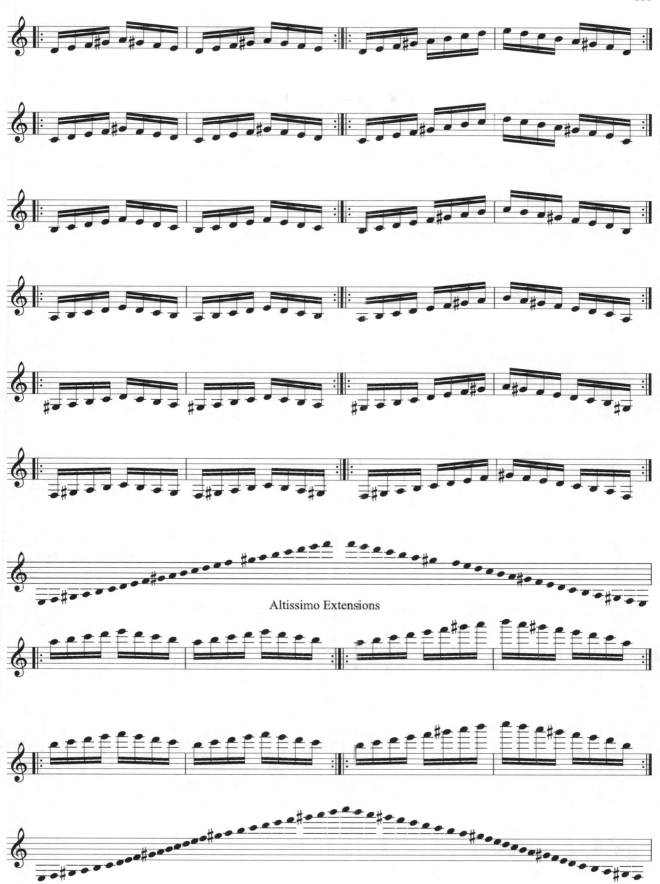

Altissimo Extensions

A   Melodic Minor

114

Bb   Harmonic Minor

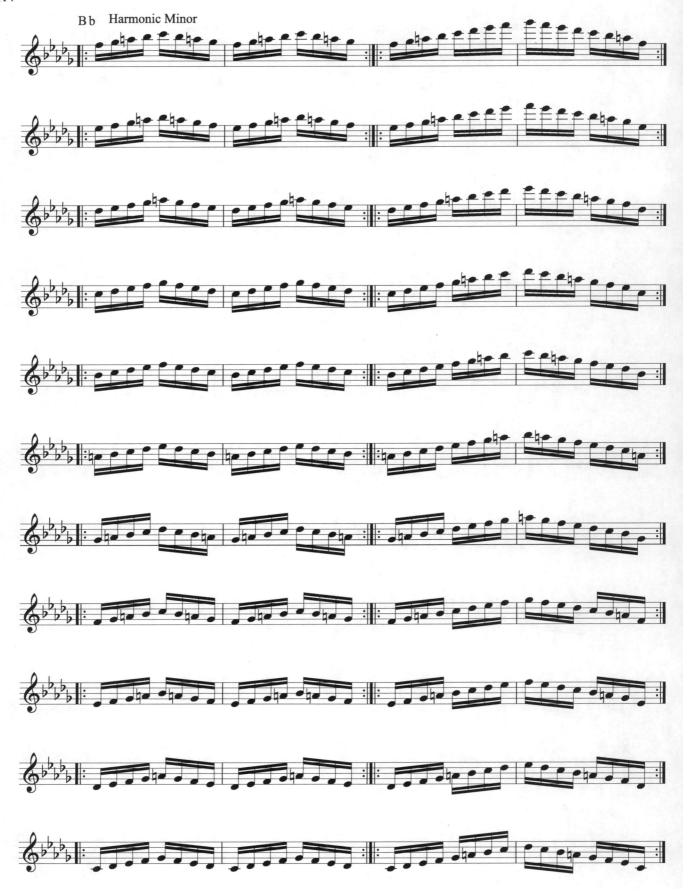

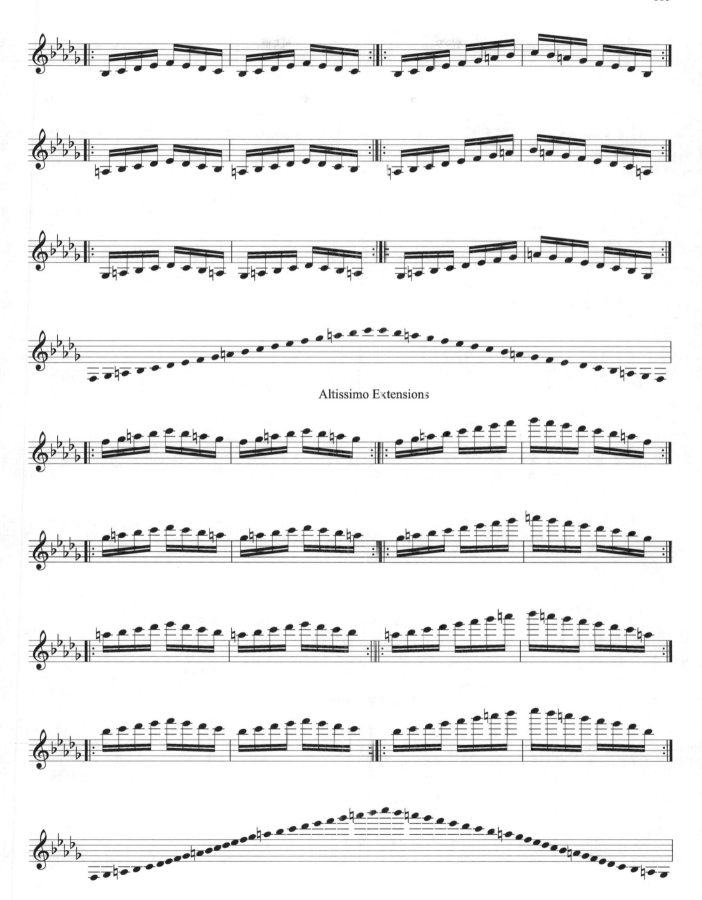

Altissimo Extensions

Bb   Melodic Minor

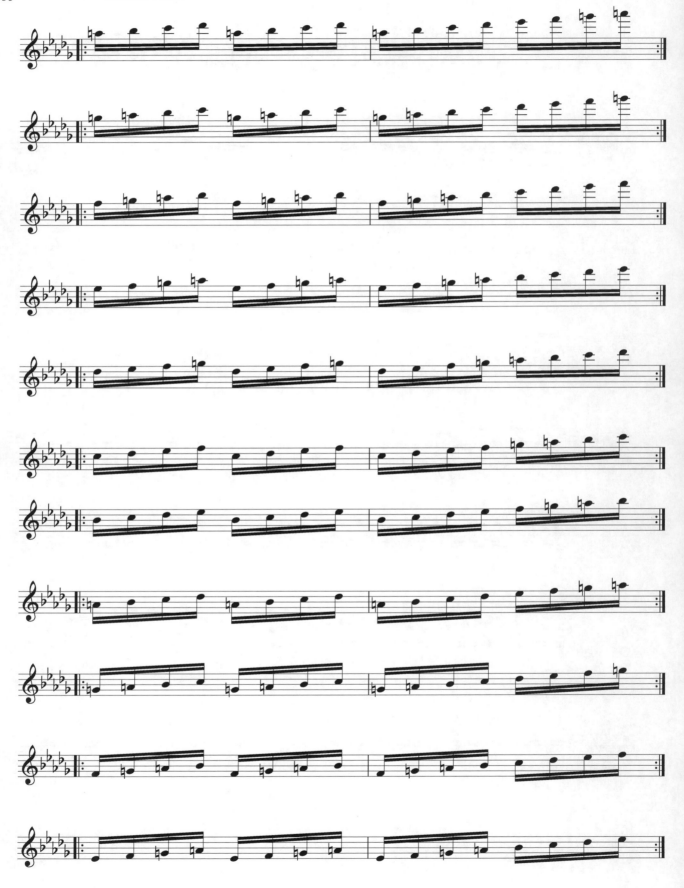

117

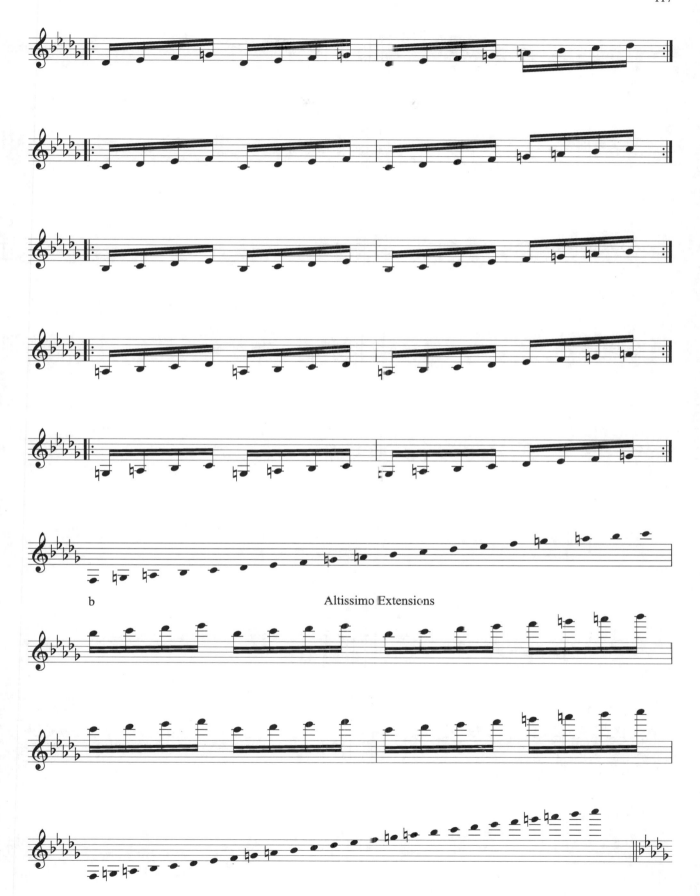

Altissimo Extensions

118

B   Harmonic Minor

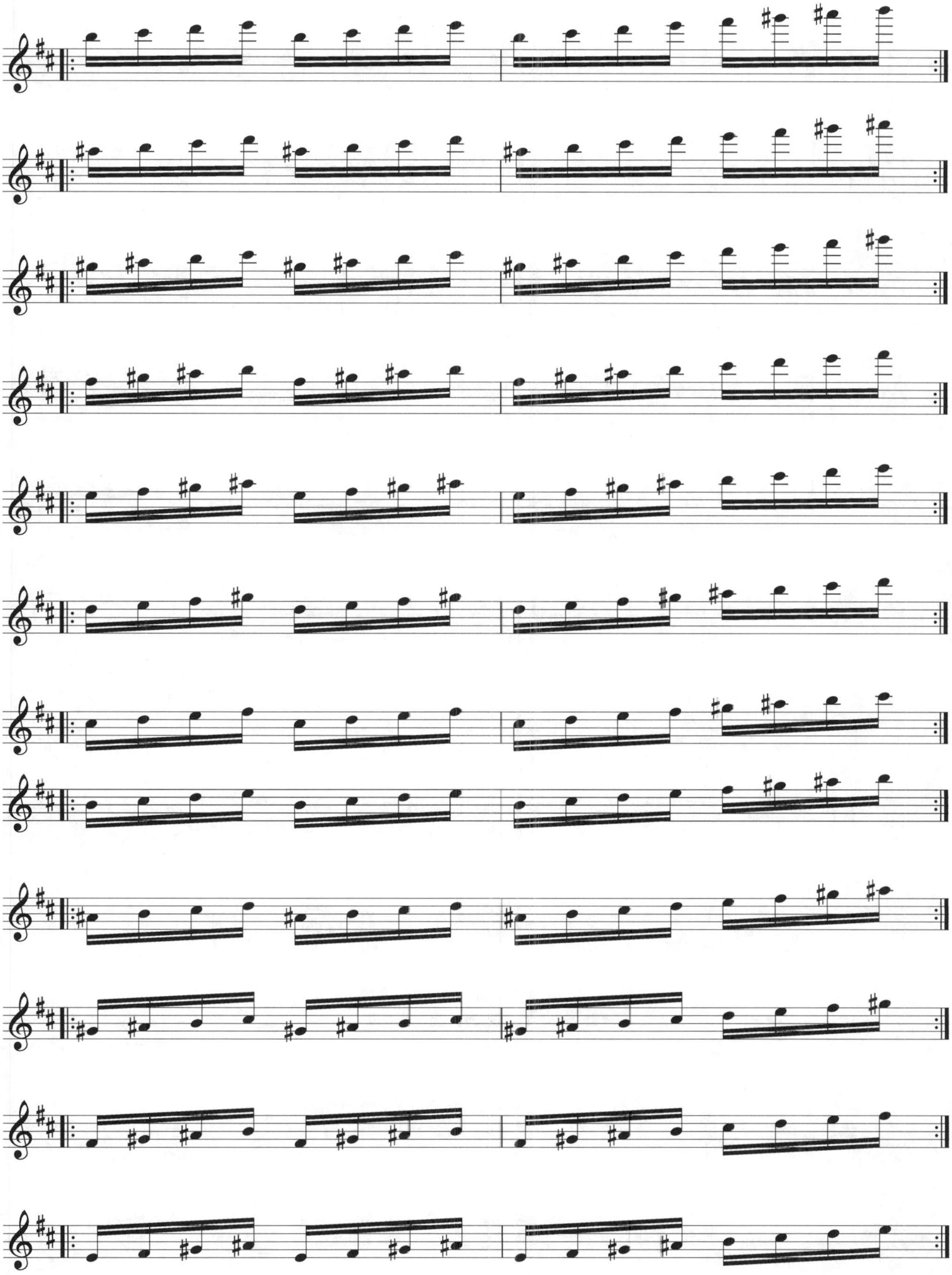

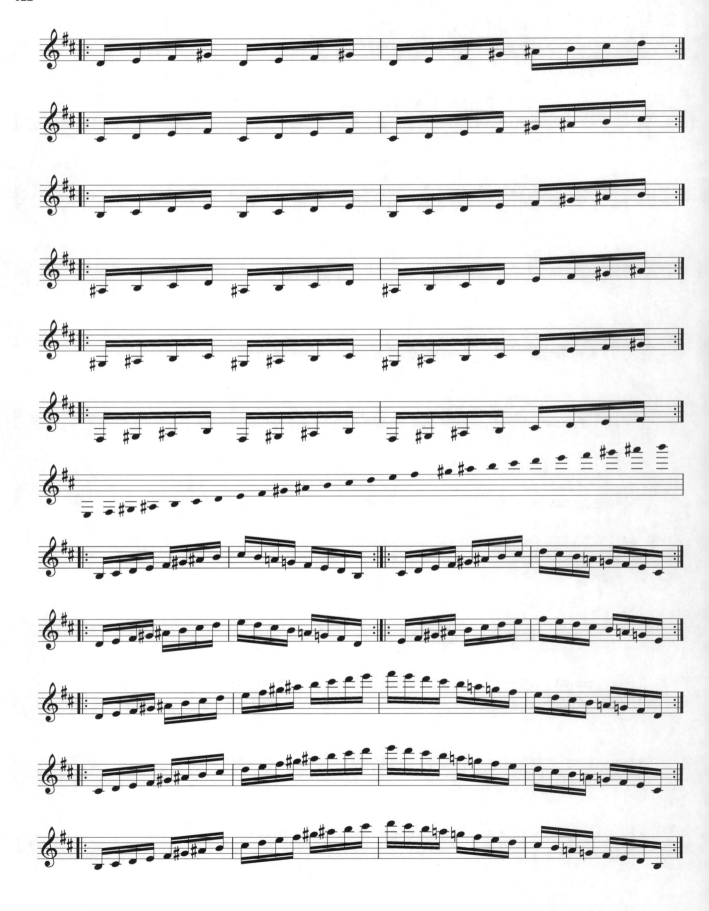

122

123

Major Chord Studies

The Appendix contains a series of Kinesthetic Chordal Studies for the _left hand_ that are an extremely useful preperation for the exercises in this section.

The sequential structure presented in the first triad (i.e., E Major) is offered in conmplete form. It should be used as the model for practicing **all** subsequent triads. All chordal studies are to be _memorized_. The short phrases (in 2/4) are **_Kinsethetic_** memory exercises. The longer sections (in 4/4/) are **conventional** memory exercises. Each series of Kinesthetic exercises should also practiced _sequentially_ as a conventional memory exercise.
The final stemless **memory sequence** should be executed seamlessly, without effort or thought!

Practice each _Kenesthetic_ exercise in groups of three _and_ six.

Conventional

Kinesthetic (Practice Kinesthetically & Sequentially)

Conventional

The two conventional exercises on this page should be played together from memory before executing the following *memory sequence*.

(Practice Kinesthetically & Sequentially)

Conventional

(Practice Kinesthetically & Sequentially)

Conventional

The two conventional exercises on this page should be played together from memory before executing the following *memory sequence*.

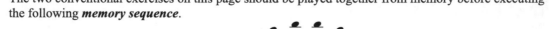

F# Major
(Practice Kinesthetically & Sequentially)

Conventional

(Practice Kinesthetically & Sequentially)

Conventional

The two conventional exercises on this page should be played together from memory before executing the following *memory sequence*.

128

Ab Major

130

A Major

Bb Major

132

B Major

C Major

136

Eb Major

Minor triads can now be practiced by repeating the major triad studies with a lowered third.
The following three triads are the only exceptions to that procedure:

Minor Chord Studies

Ab Minor

138

A Minor

C Minor

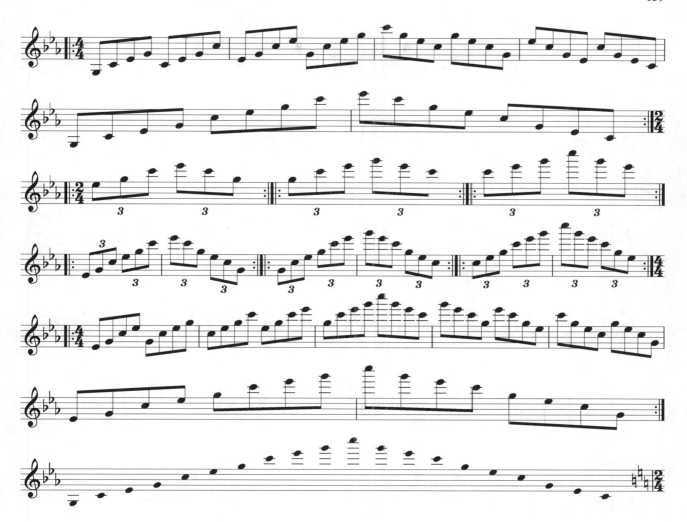

DOMINANT SEVENTH CHORD STUDIES

Remember, Kinesthetic exercises (i.e., exercises in 2/4) must also be practised
sequentially as conventional memory exercises!

Altissimo Extensions

142

F Dom 7

144

F# Dom7

G Dom

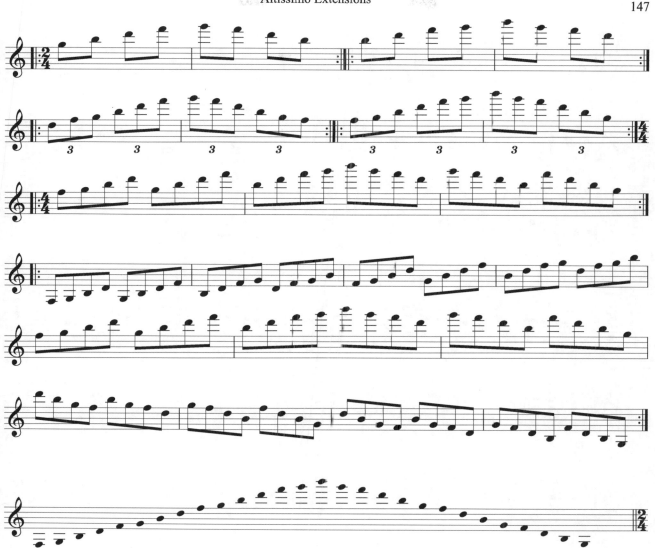

148

Ab Dom

150

A Dom

A Dom

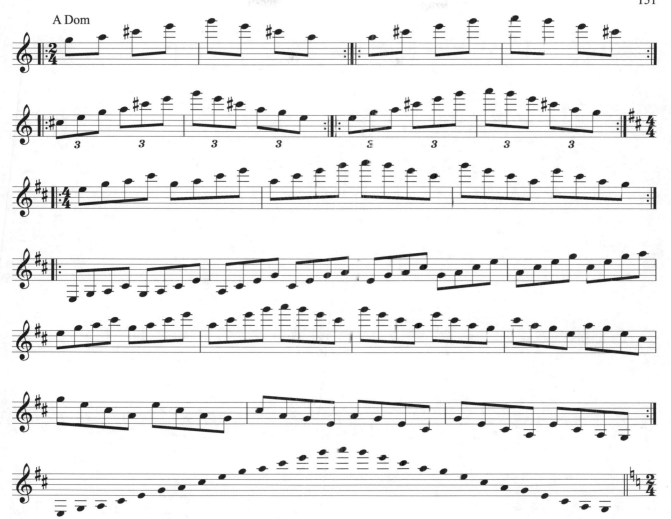

152

Bb Dom

154

156

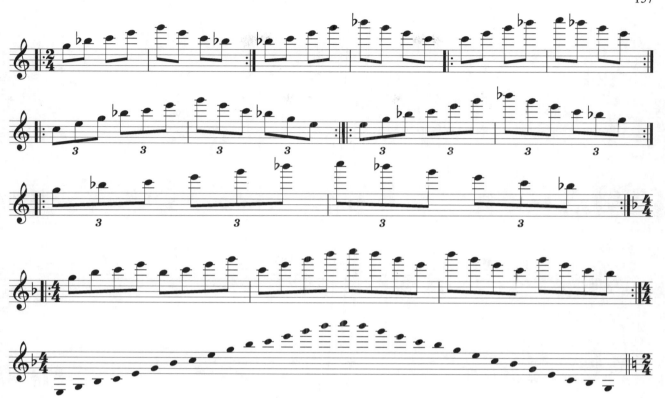

158

C# Dom

Altissimo Extensions

160

Eb   Dom

Diminished Seventh Chord Studies

Altissimo Extensions

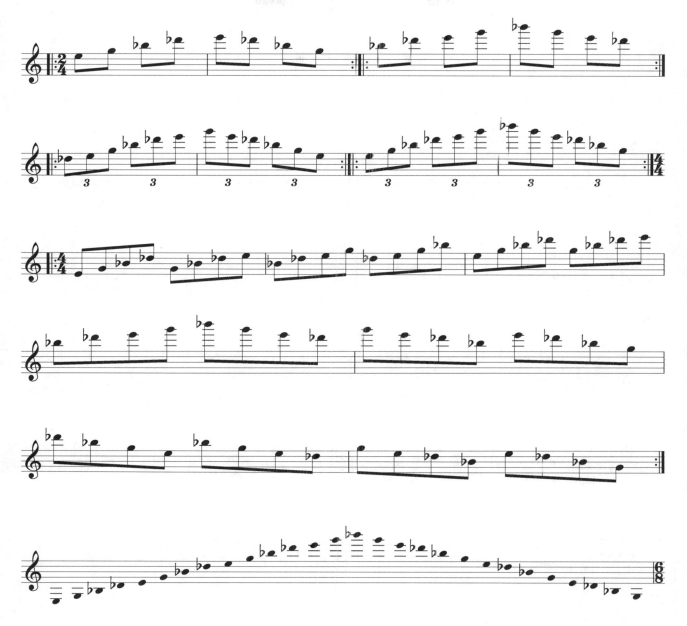

Diminished Scale Studies

166

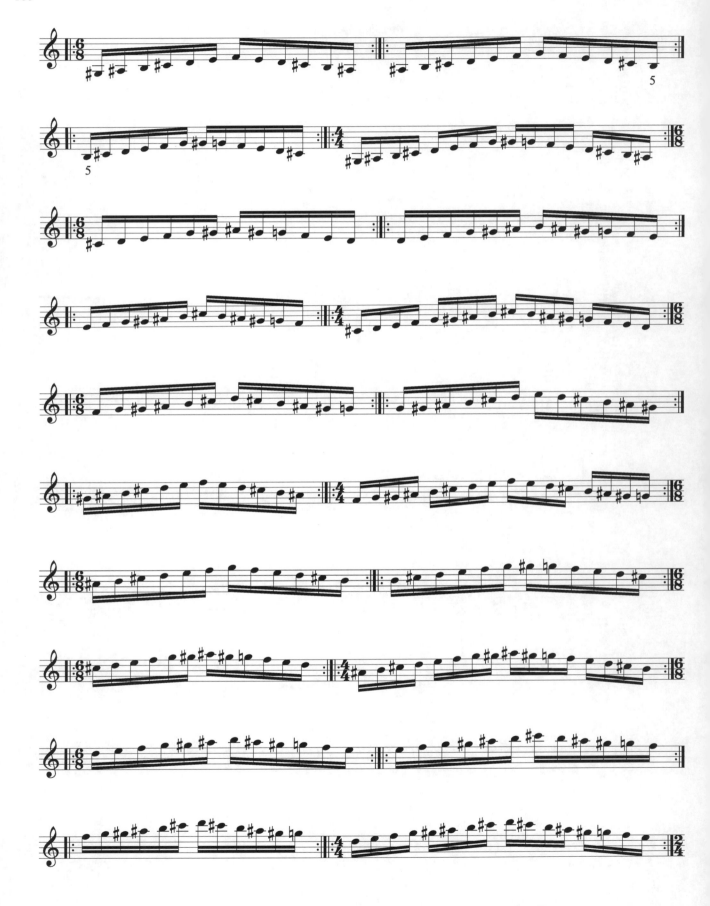

Altissimo Extensions

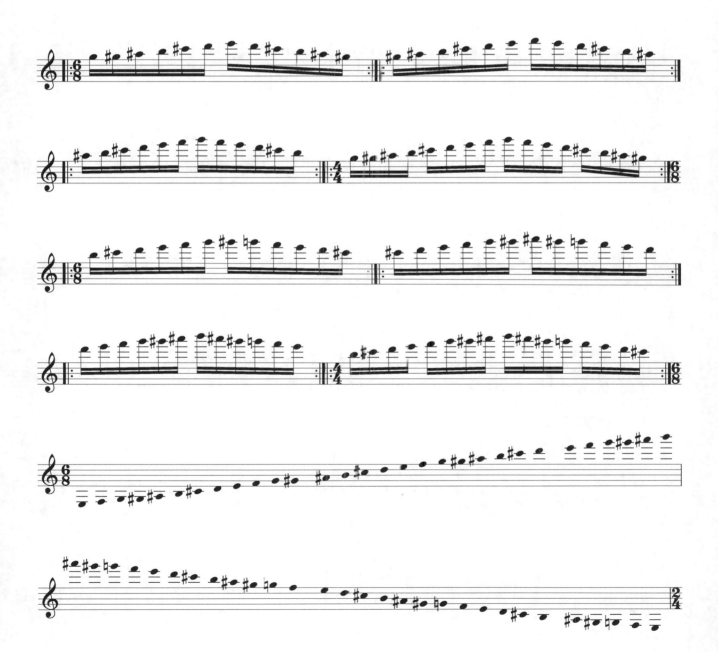

168

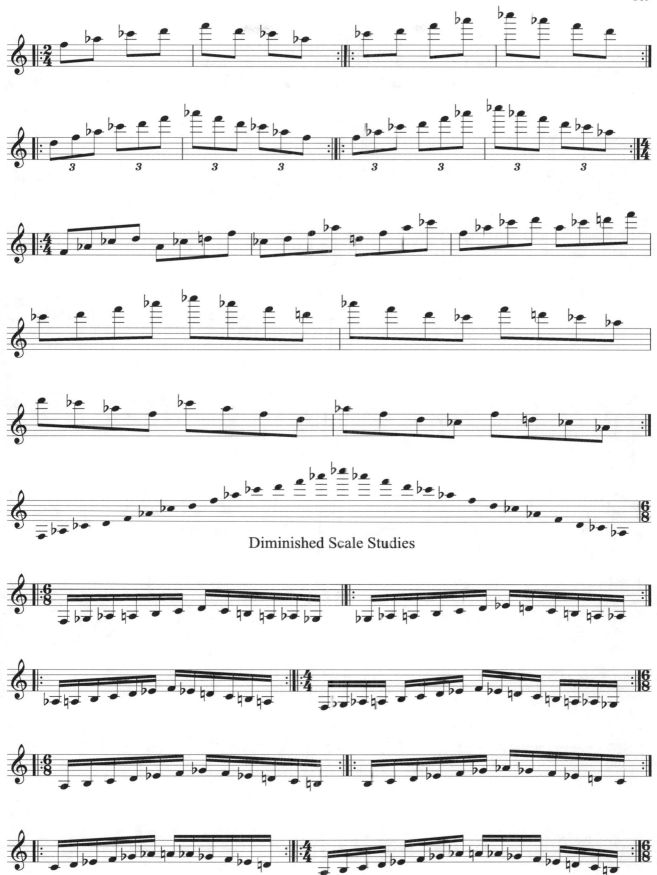

Diminished Scale Studies

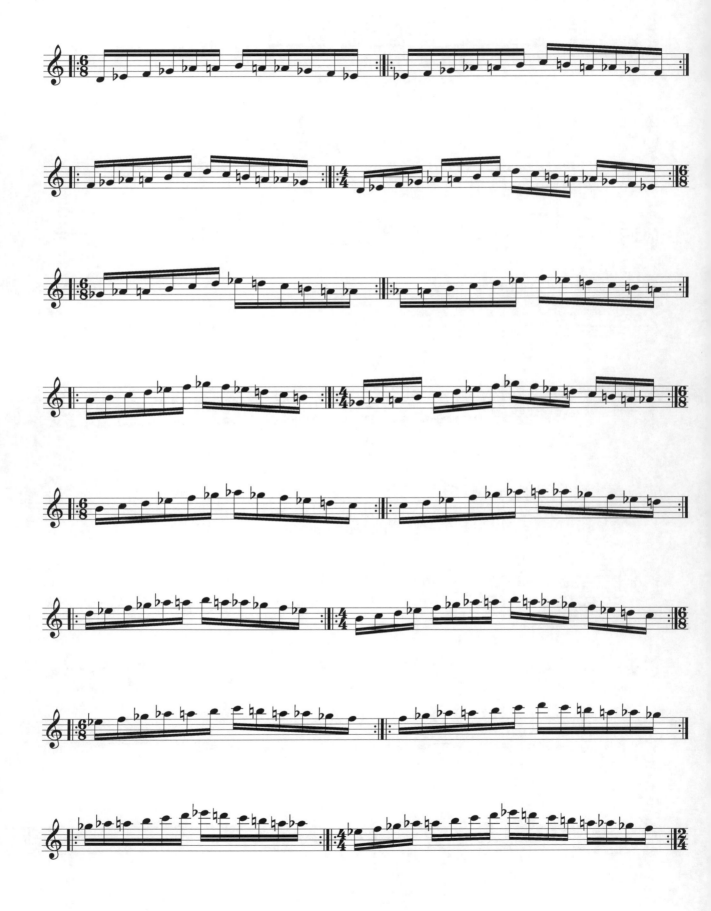

Altissimo Extensions

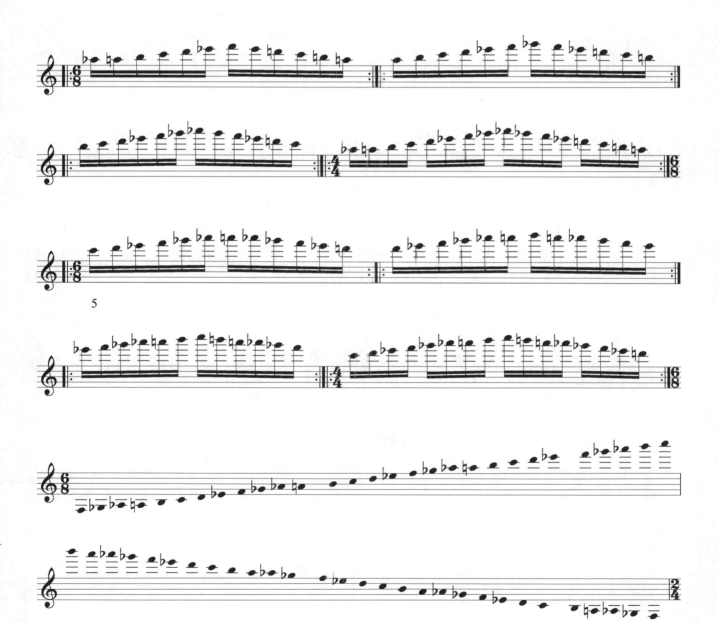

5

172

Diminished Scale Studies

174

Major Scales for Daily Review

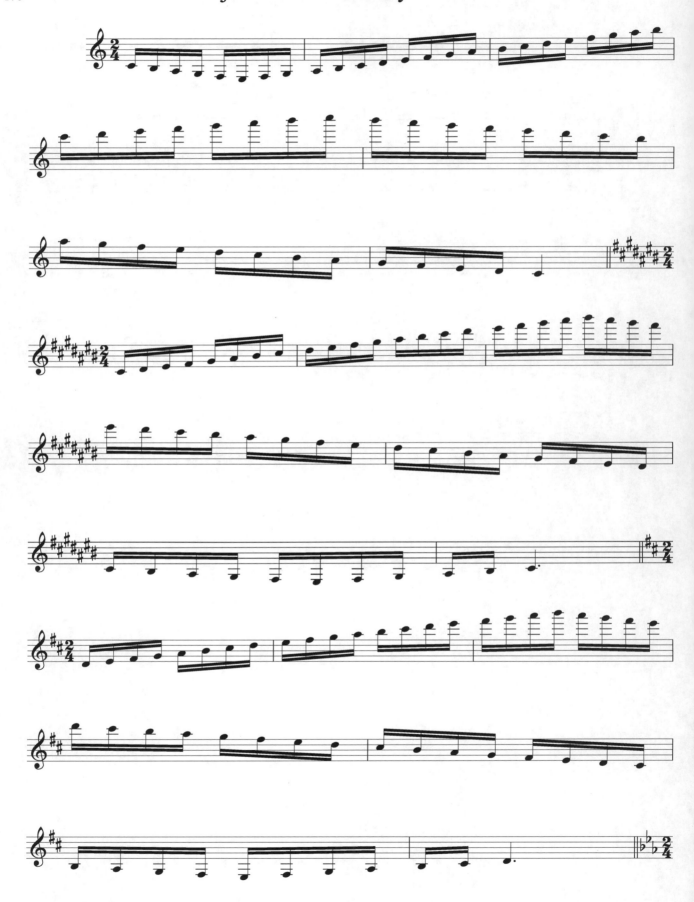

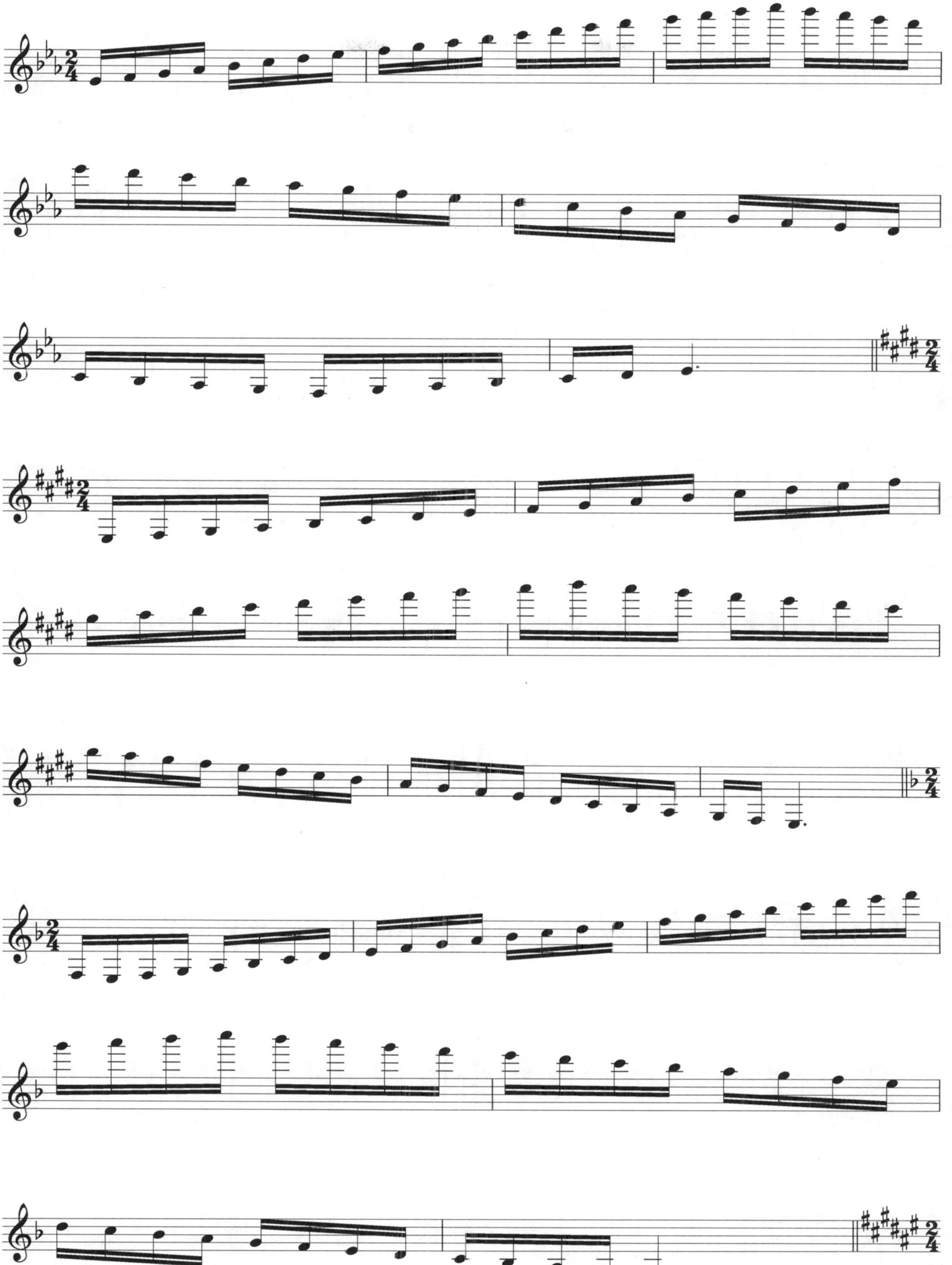

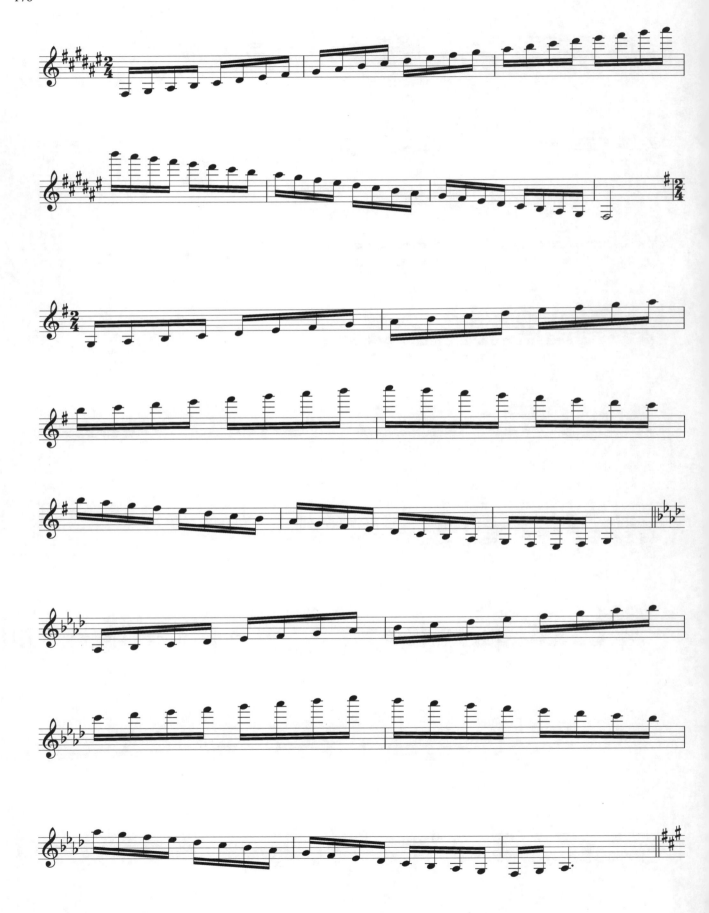

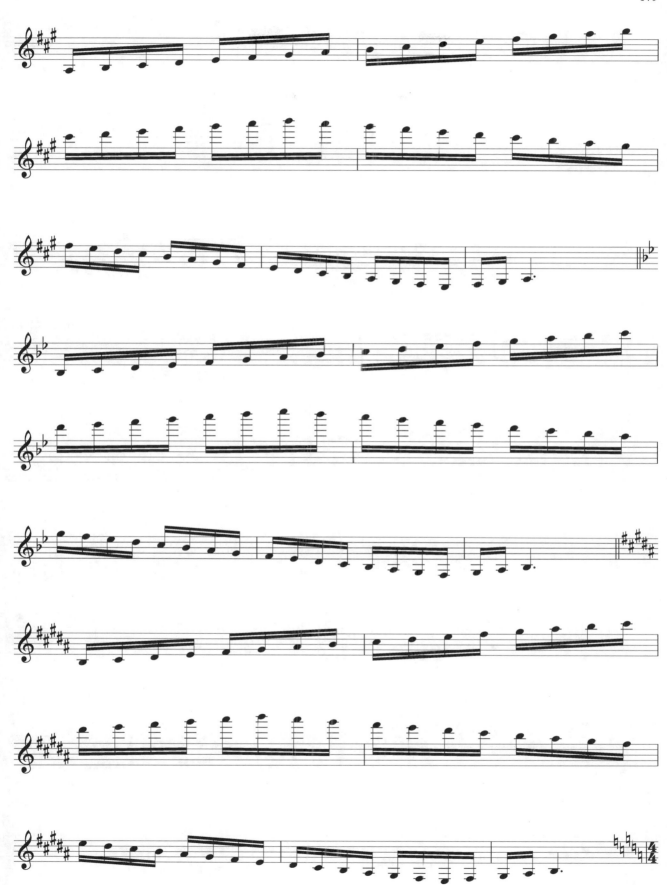

Major Scales in Thirds

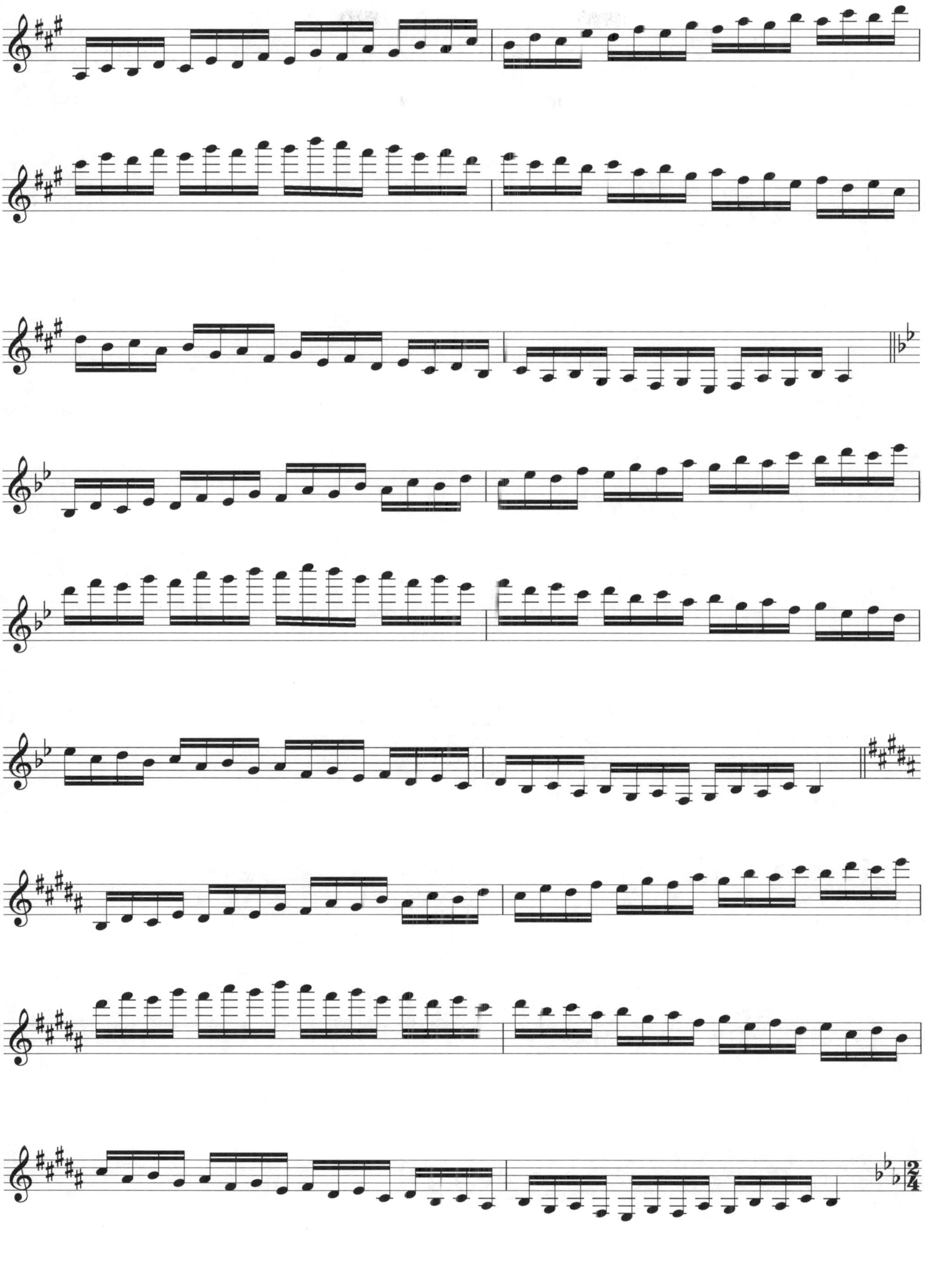

Minor Scales For Daily Revue
Melodic Minor

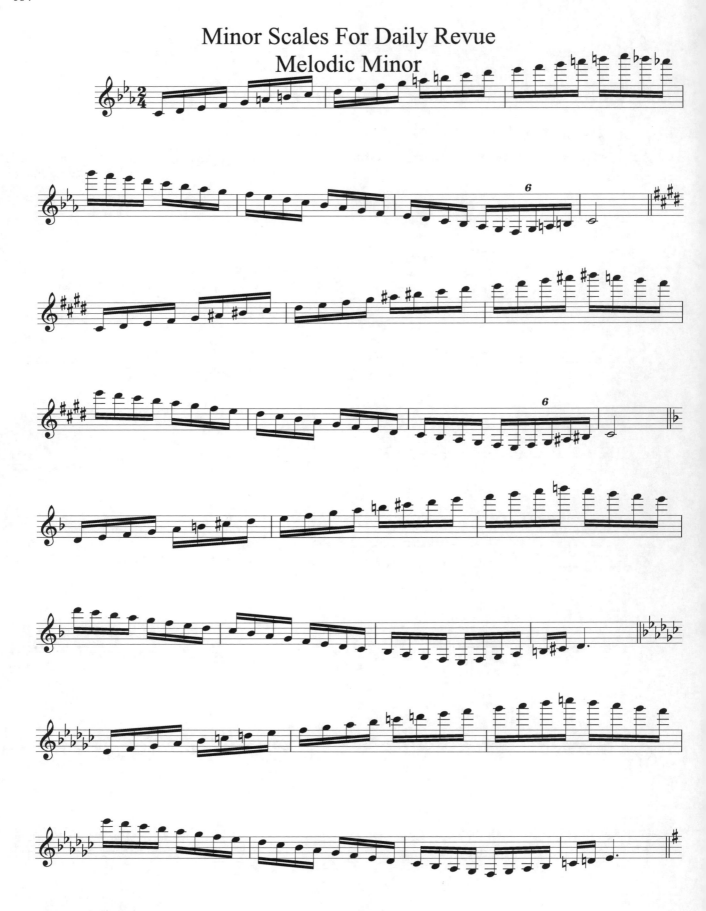

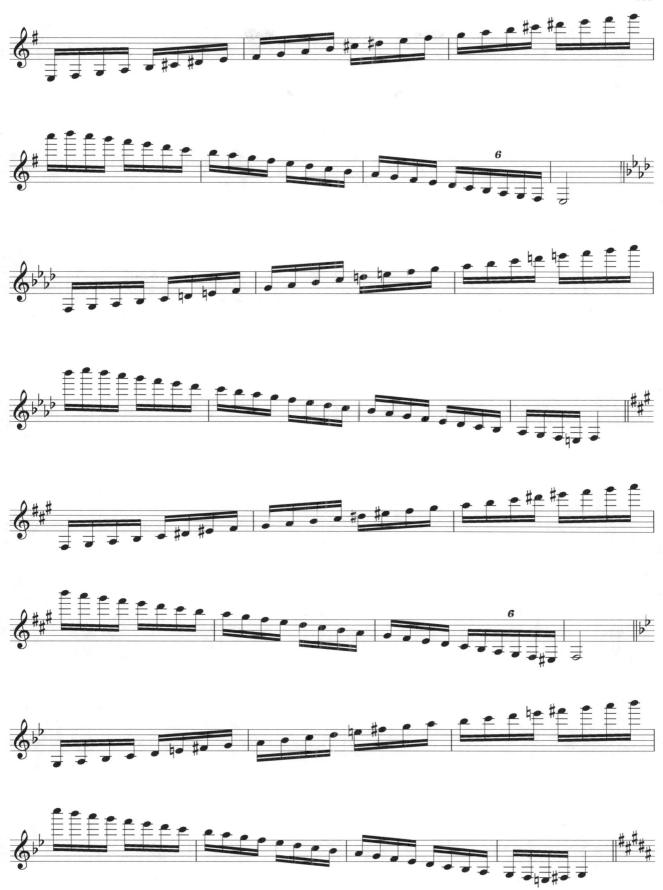

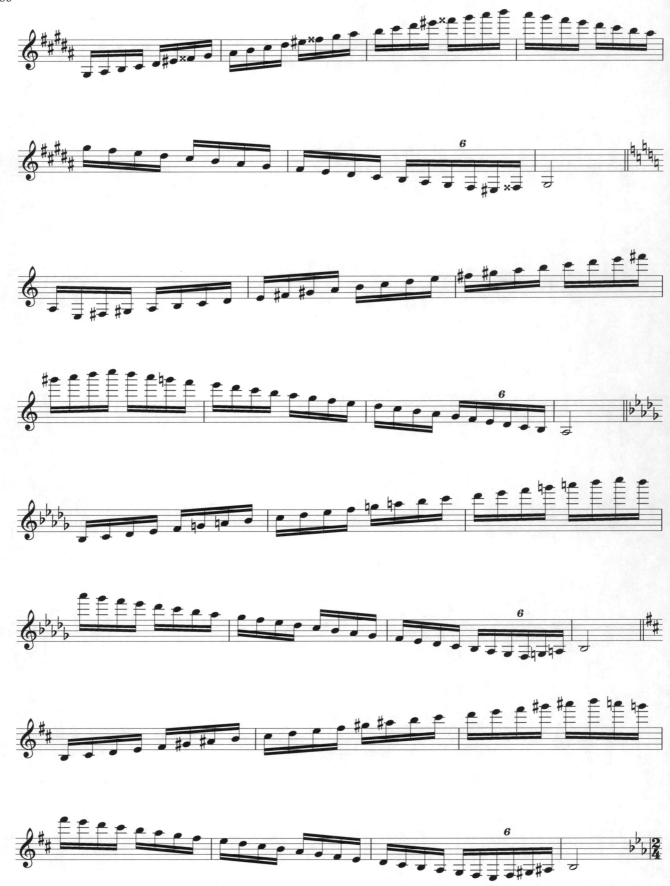

Melodic Minor Scales in Thirds

Harmonic Minor

191

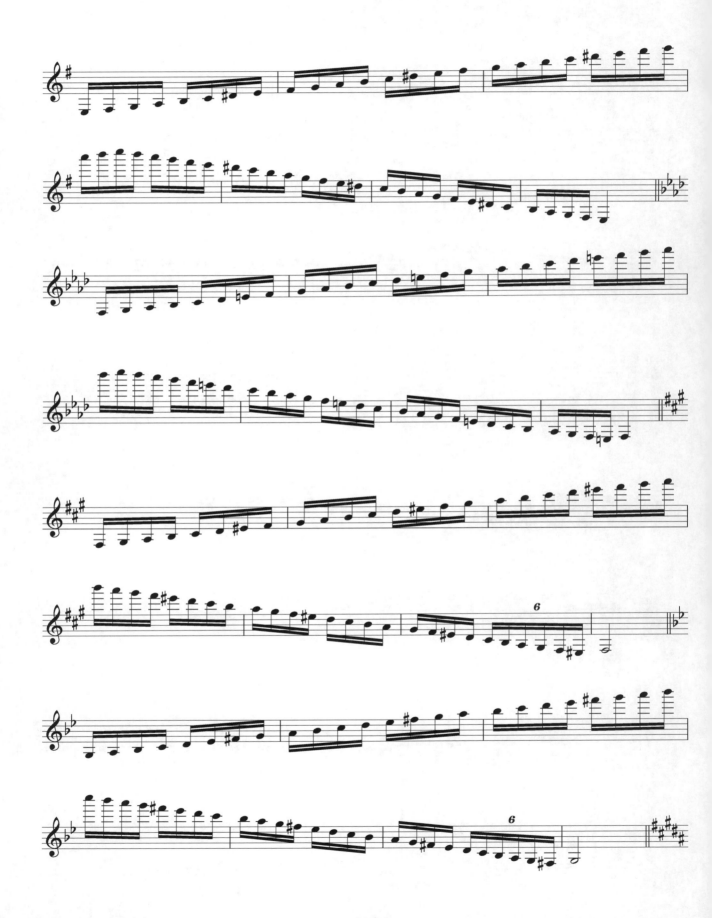

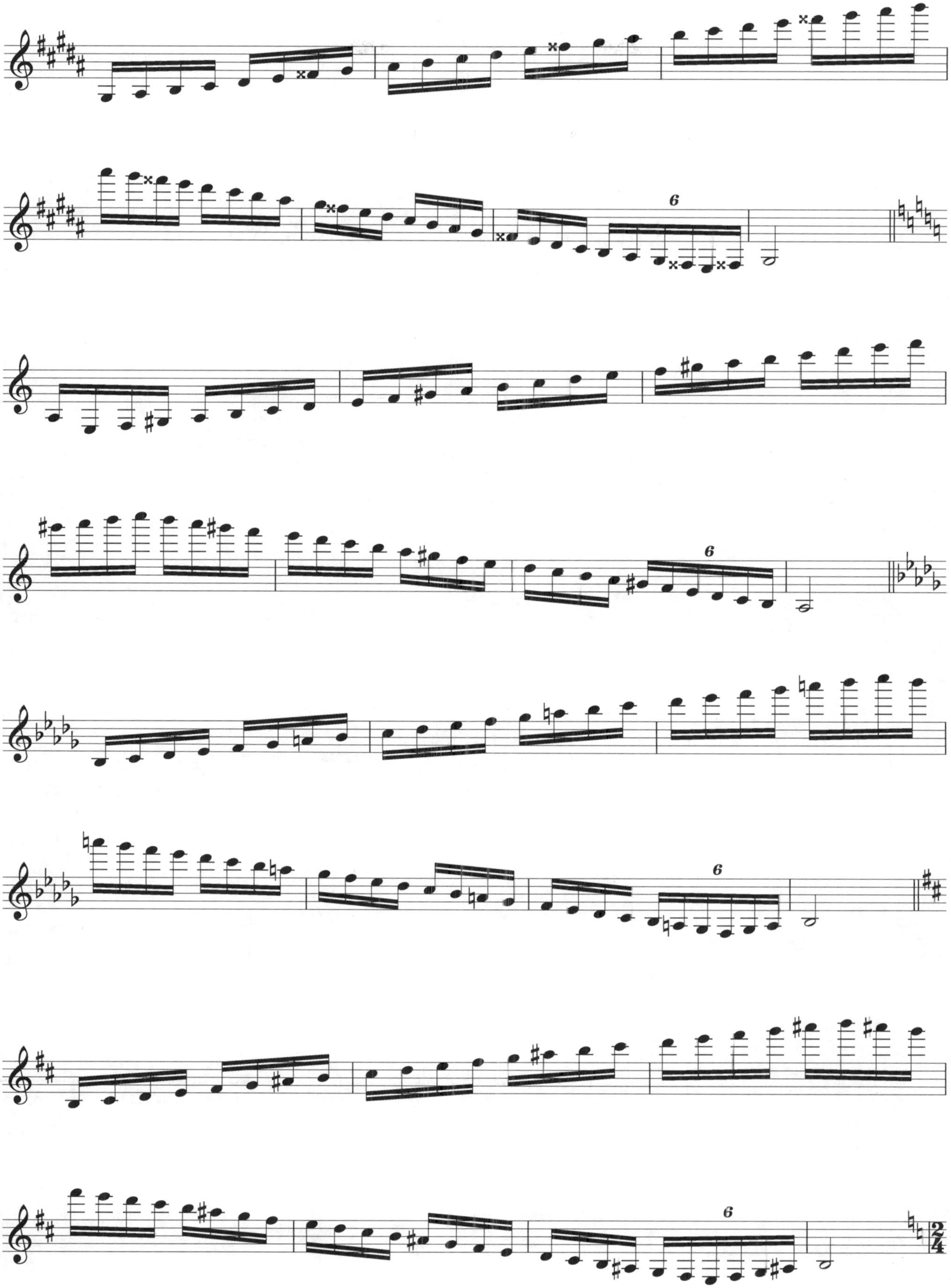

Diminished Scales For Daily Review

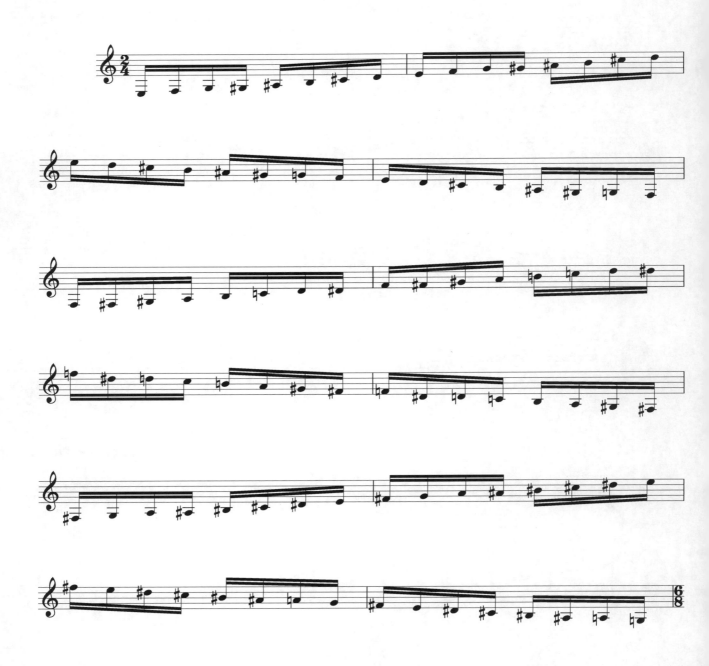

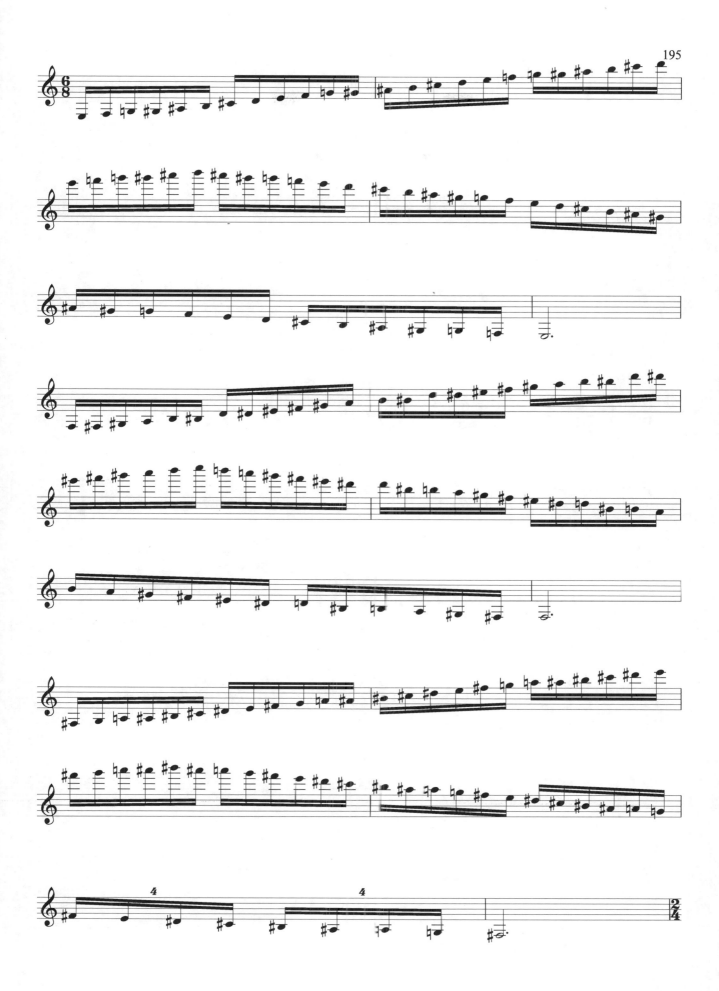

Chords For Daily Practice
Major Triads

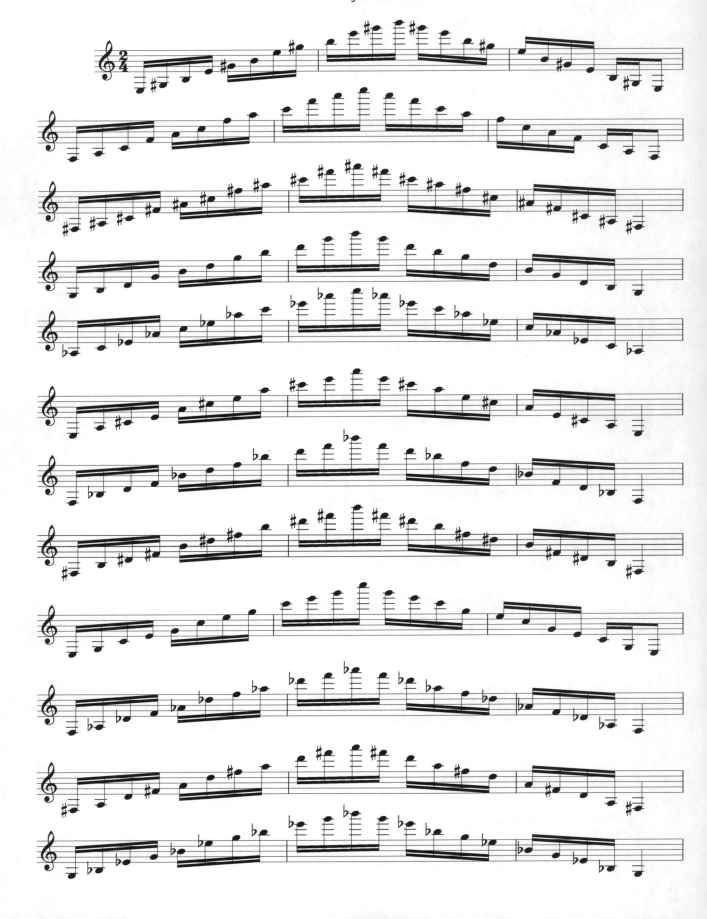

Minor Triads

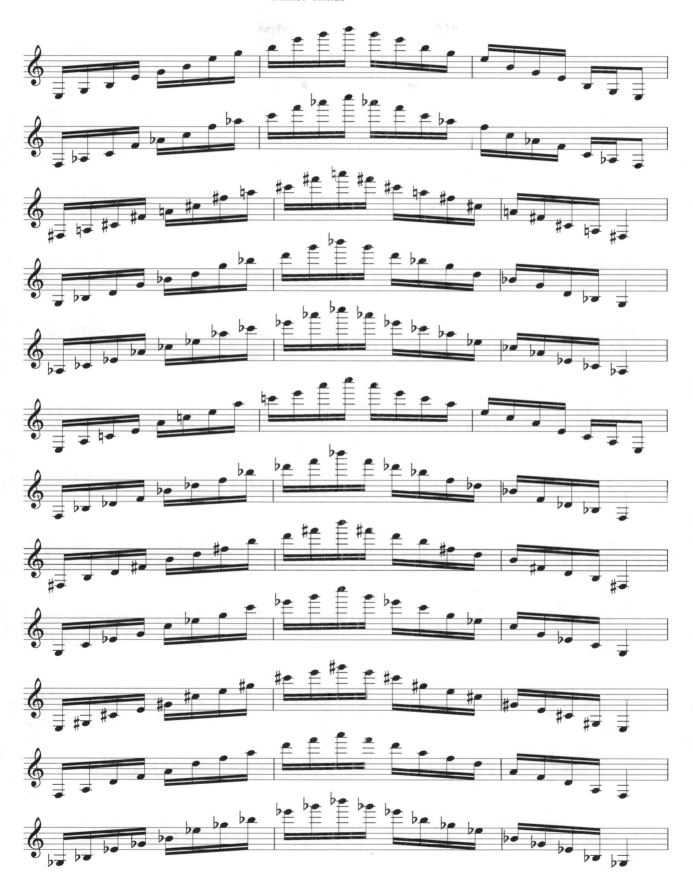

Dominant Seventh Chords

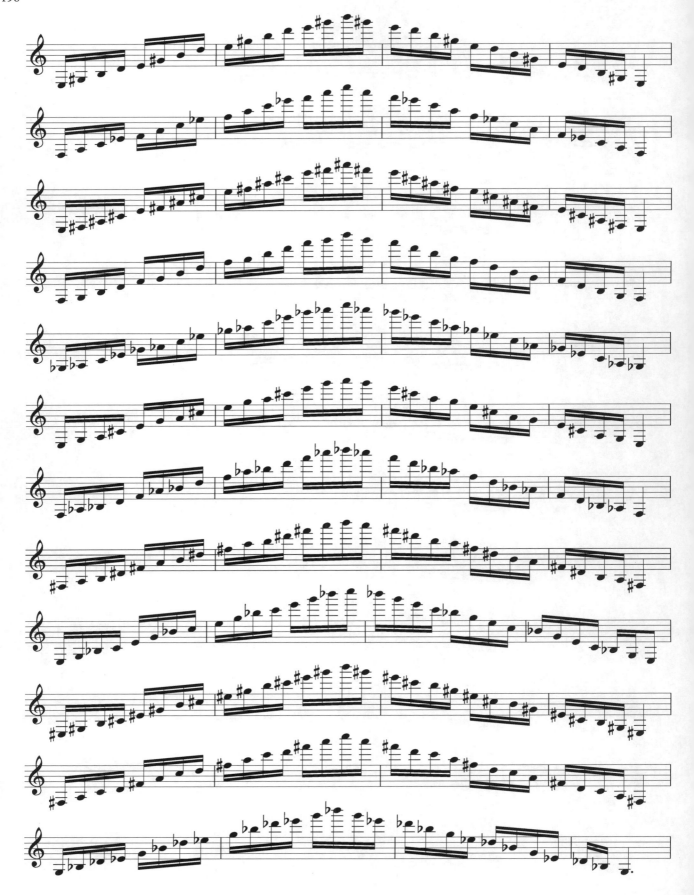

Dominuished Seventh Chords

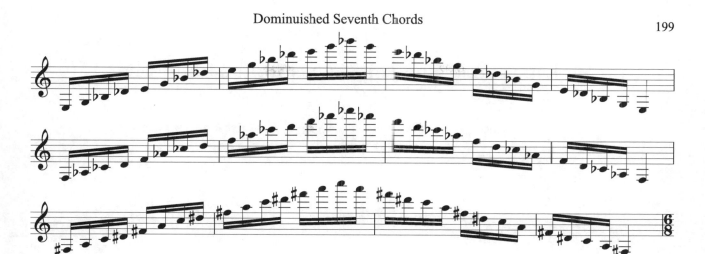

Appendix

Kinesthetic Chordal Studies for the Left Hand

Each <u>measure</u> should be practiced as a *separate* **Kinesthic Memory** exercise.

Major

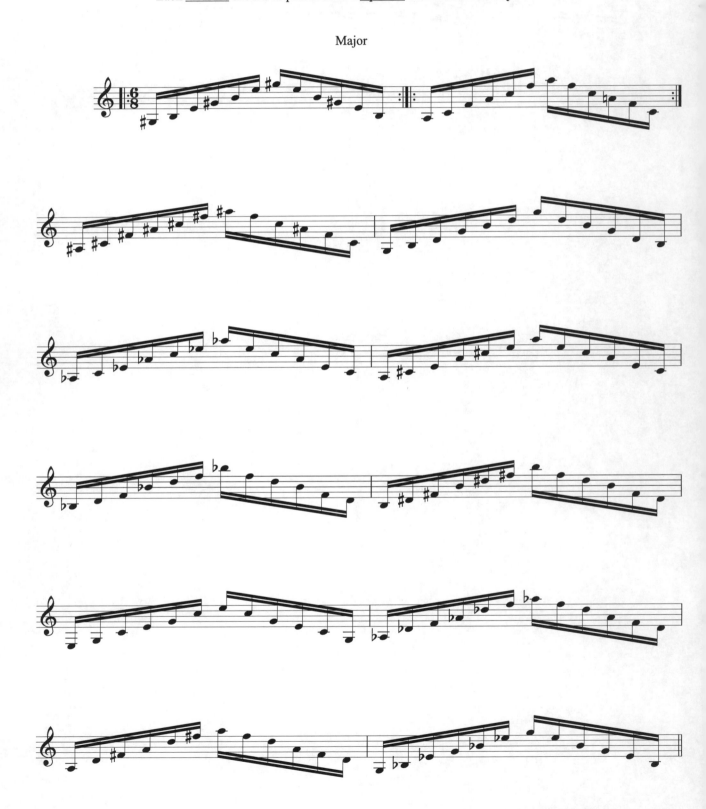

Minor

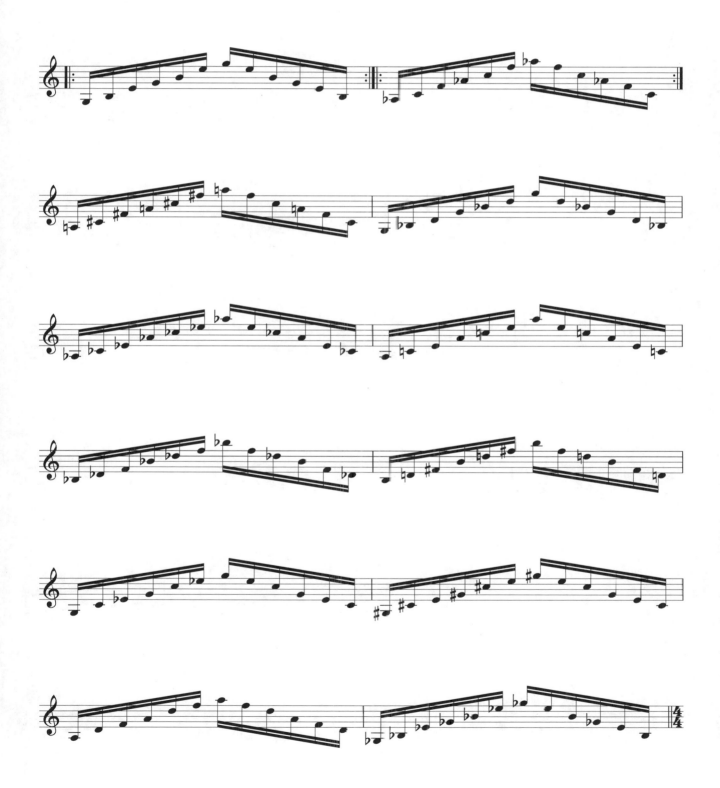

202

Dominant Seventh

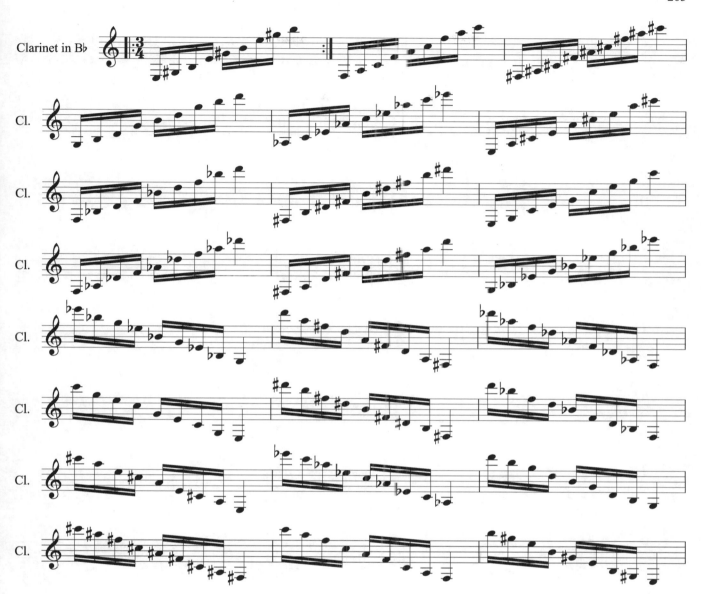

Minor

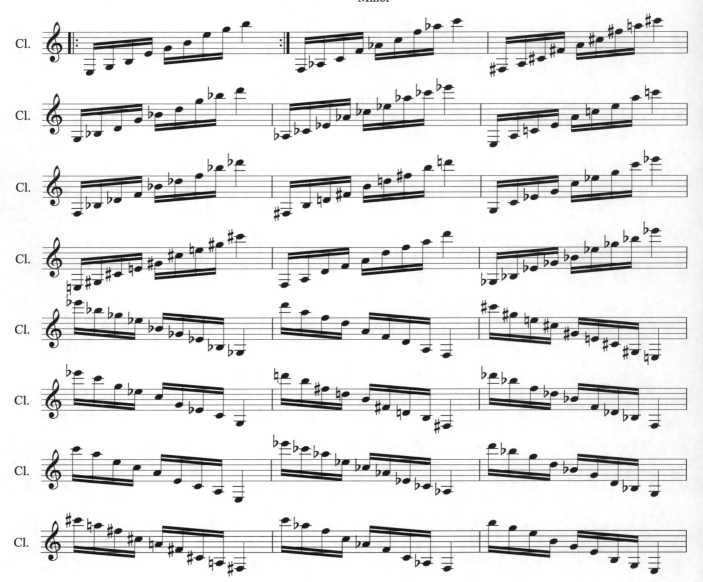

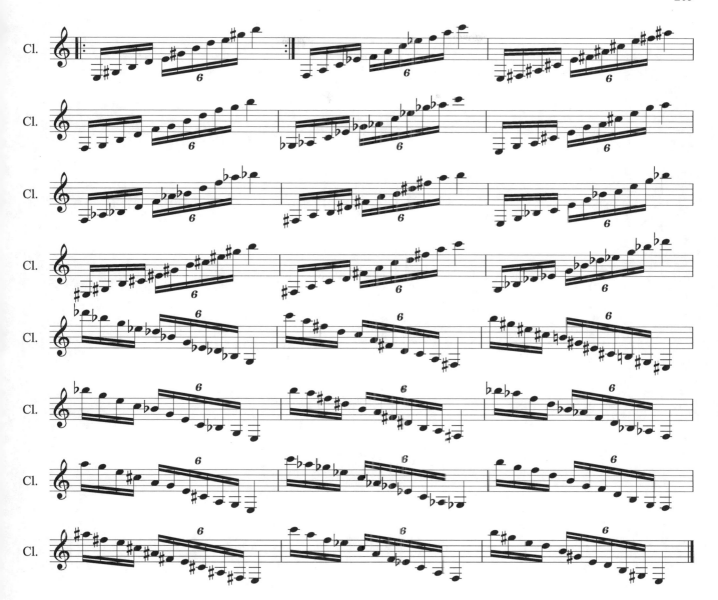

DEXTERITY STUDIES

&
EXERCISES

For
The Clarinet

Book Two

DEXTERITY STUDIES

By
Valdea D. Jennings, BS Mus. Ed. Ed.D.

Introduction

Book II is divided into two parts. Part I contains 100 discrete exercises. Part II offers a series if longer exercises.

The patterns in both parts are designed to facilitate the use of selected keys singly and in combination. It is hoped that the complexity of the fingering combinations will promote both accuracy and dexterity. Fingering suggestions have not been supplied; in most instances they are dictated by the patterns themselves. When there are options, the choice is left to the discretion of the teacher. However if any passage can be played in more than one to manner, it is suggested that they be learned and played in all! For optimal effect, the exercises should _not_ be edited, that is, no fingerings should be written in. This should insure that the exercises will initially be played **slowly**. Also, this means that difficult combinations and transitions must be _remembered_.

In many instances, key signatures have been omitted. This was done in an effort to reduce the complexity of the reading task, thus allowing the student to focus on the execution of the fingering patterns. The intent is to facilitate learning by making use of kinesthesia, i.e., the active awareness of the movement and positioning of the fingers in the repetitive playing of this and other exercises. With this in mind, difficult transitions and sequences should be extracted in short segments and practiced as **Kinesthetic Memory Exercises**. Careful attention should always be paid to finger positioning, limiting both motion and distance from the rings.

Valdea D. Jennings, BS Music Ed., Ed. D.

100 Daily Dexterity Exercises

Valdea D. Jennings, Ed. D.

6

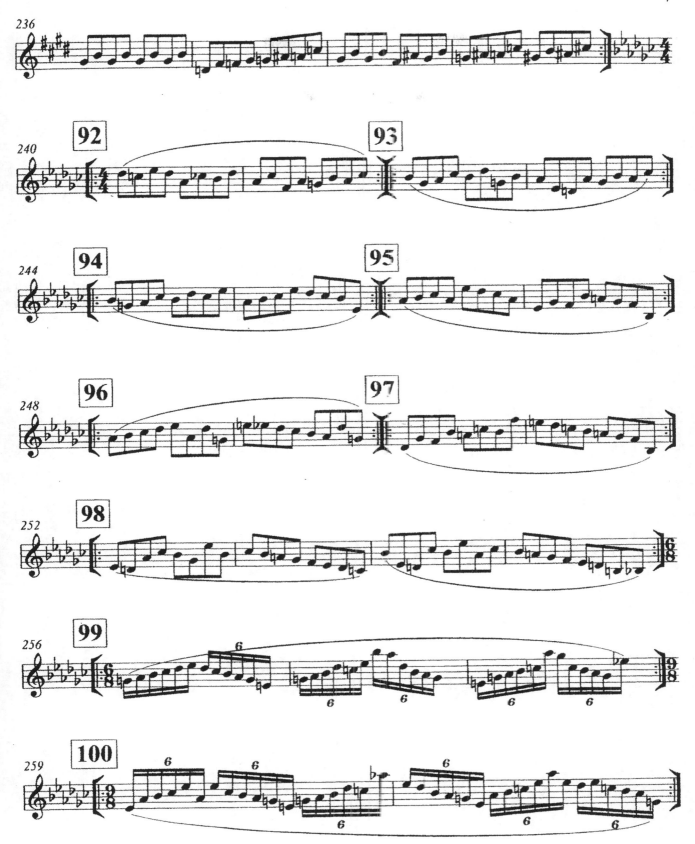

7

Five Dexterity Studies
No. 1

Valdea D. Jennings Ed.D

No.2

NO.3

No. 4

Valdea D. Jennings, Ed. D

No. 5
To be played both legato & staccato

An Exercise For The 18th Key

Left hand Eb/Ab key to be used where marked (*)

Valdea D. Jennings, Ed. D.

Exercise For ForkFingerings

ValdeaD.Jennings,Ed.D.